The Truth:

THE REAL SECRET TO BUILDING A BUSINESS THAT SETS YOU FREE

Dr.Tony Pennells
& Makaylah Rogers

CONTENTS

PART III
YOUR NEXT STEPS

CHAPTER 11

INTRODUCTION

The book you're holding in your hands right now is not *information.*

It is a *REVOLUTION.*

We imagine you may have started your business to make a difference in the world, to make great money and to make money in a way that feels more freedom based. No more clocking in at 9 and clocking out at 5.

The appeal of business is obvious, yet so many business owners have the appearance of success and live a reality that isn't pretty. The reality is that most suffer with a roller coaster of inconsistent cash flow and have amassed huge levels of debt to get to where they are. They feel the need to keep up appearances because they don't feel they can truly share the difficulties they face.

While you likely chose to build a business to get out of the trap of the 9 to 5, sadly the fact is that most business owners are 50% worse off than employees at the end of their working life. It's shocking yet true.

We've created this book as part of our revolution. We're devoted to changing this statistic. The only way out is to become Financially Free.

Let us define Financial Freedom because it's likely not what you think. It's the reality of having enough money coming in outside of your business so when the time comes that you can't work anymore, you have enough money coming in. This reality must be in place when you can no longer work.

So the way we see it is, if you have to create this reality anyway, why not create it sooner?

As a business owner, you're in a unique position. You have a greater opportunity to become Free, because there is no ceiling on the amount of money you can create.

In order to do this, we need to end some of the bullshit that has created a reality of financial stress and struggle in so many business owners lives.

The Reality Behind The Appearance of Success

Growing up, I (Makaylah) was able to see the contrasts of "success" mixed with financial stress, turmoil and overwhelming debt. I realized I didn't want my life to turn out the same. Not only that, I didn't want to just follow the standard career path most people took.

I had no idea "what I wanted to do when I grew up" because I didn't see that what I wanted to do really fitted in with what the career guidance counsellors at school told me I could do.

I felt a deep calling inside to create change. To leave the world better then how I found it.

I wanted to see different behaviours in the world then what I currently saw was normal.

I wanted to create a legacy, to be the catalyst of major movements in the world.

Such as the extinction of sexual, physical and emotional abuse of children, to eliminate poverty worldwide and get every human being off the street to having their basic human needs met. I wanted to revolutionise the education system so that my children and grandchildren didn't go through the same system I did.

People like Oprah inspired me. I saw her as someone who was creating massive impact in the world. She had wealth, freedom, influence and an abundance of money. I also saw that she understood that money itself wasn't the end game. That is was simply a means for her to create the greatest possible change and impact in the world, which is what she was doing. I wanted to be like her. To have the freedom of time and choice to follow whatever calling I had and have the resources to back it.

I saw pretty early on that money would accelerate the impact I could create in the world, I wanted to be someone who had the influence and money to create big change. (That wasn't something that was on the list of university degrees I could get.)

I truly believe that the biggest impact we can make happens when we don't *need* to work for money. That only then will our fullest creative potential open up. And only then is it possible for us to fulfill the highest vision for the impact we're capable of creating in this world. Financial need creates a fog that limits our fullest potential from ever being seen, let alone realized.

Now, you might be thinking that you don't need money to create change. I believe that money gives you greater ability to change things in the world around you, faster. Imagine you had ten times the advertising budget you do now, wouldn't that help you reach people faster? The world does revolve around money, so I decided to get on board with that and do everything I could to create the abundance in my life that could ripple and affect millions. I set out to do just that and started on a very intense 2 year journey where I realised two very important lessons that I hope will help you on your journey. I'll share those in a moment.

The first was that I discovered that if I wanted to impact millions and create global change, I'd need to make sure I was taken care of first. Airplanes have instructions to place your oxygen mask on first before placing someone else's on. The reason is because you can't help others if you're dead.

I made the decision I was going to build my wealth and put my oxygen mask on first and then help others do the same, so they could also make the impact they were born to make in the world. By 18 I began building my "cash bucket" (net savings).

I started building a direct sales company and had acquired team and customer internationally within 6 months. I became a keynote speaker. Within a year I was deputy CEO of one company and building my career as a 19 year-old woman in real estate, surrounded by male realtors mostly over 50. I was truly on track for the "success" I had envisioned. The people around me were amazed at what I was able to create.

Then, within a period of just 8 months I got severely sick and couldn't even work at all. I had to use all of the money I had saved just to get by. If it wasn't for my family I may not have even survived. This is when I learned the second important lesson during those two years.

I could see that creating wealth and abundance wasn't enough on it's own. Money meant nothing if I had to sacrifice my health in order to make it. I knew I needed more. I finally got that I didn't have to wait until I made the money to create the impact. I asked myself "What if I can do both now? Build my Freedom AND live in passion, service and fulfillment today?"

As I started getting better I knew I needed to build my Freedom and wealth in a way that was in alignment with the impact I wanted to create now, not just in the future.

It was at that time that I met Dr. Tony Pennells at the second seminar he ever conducted, which was where we both lived at the time in Perth, Western Australia. Tony had built multiple 7-figure companies, he was Financially Free at 27 years old, yet he wasn't arrogant or showy like the examples of success I we see in our society. He simply asked the audience profound questions and had an presence of true service to others.

I listened and finally felt like someone was telling me the truth, not speaking for some bullshit pitch at the end. I saw something crucial that I was missing in my plan. That I needed to make my money work for me, to get cash flow from my investments, not just grow a cash bucket and building "wealth" as many speak of it. I realized that cash flow was the only thing that would pay my bills, give me freedom and fund what I had envisioned.

After his talk, I interviewed Tony. Our 15-minute call turned into an hour. What Tony said on this call inspired me, it shattered my old way of thinking about money and opened me up to an entirely new world: a world that I could have, that would enable me to make my Oprah-Like-Impact I'd always desired.

He said he was done with playing small. And then he said something that became the seed of the Revolution you're holding in your hands now.

He said, "I want to create a new normal in society. One where it's MORE normal to be financially free (making enough money through cash flow investments to pay for our basic living expenses) than it is to work for money... I know how to build multi-million dollar businesses and I've taught others how to as well, but I want to create something that impacts the world 10, 20, 30 times what I can even imagine. I want to know that the world I leave my kids is better then the one I lived."
He was speaking my language.

After that, Tony asked me to propose how I saw myself helping him bring that mission into reality. In all the multiple 7 figure business's he had created, he said he had never seen someone as naturally skilled and capable as me in building business's that created social change.

Through our vision for change, my ambitious drive to create powerful movements in the world, my skills in bringing powerful visions to life and Tony's experience in building and selling 7-figure businesses in a way that creates Financial Freedom, we developed the philosophy you're about to learn in this book.

It's the process we created together, and the process we use every day in building MindShift.money – which aims to change the way every person on the planet thinks about money, starting with a tipping point of 20 million people.

What you're about to learn.

During our time together in PART I of this book, you're going to learn WHY creating Financial Freedom is absolutely necessary to not only take care of yourself in the future, but to also realize your fullest potential to create a massive impact in the world. You'll also learn how you can set your business up to create the greatest impact it can, in a way that feels aligned with who you are as you build towards unleashing your fullest potential. You're also going to bust through some devastating *"Money Myths"* that hold so many people back from creating the Freedom they deserve. These are old ideas and conditioning we've been exposed to that have us setting ourselves and our financial reality up in a way that's extremely limiting. These old views have strangled society to the point where 96% of our population never become Financially Free in their lifetime and most will not have near enough money to support themselves when they can no longer work.

We've been taught that trading our time for money is *normal*; that working endless hours and running on the treadmill of business is *acceptable*. We're praised for "being busy" and given accolades for long, hard work. At MindShift.money, we call bullshit on what we've been told that has led us to where we are today.

In Chapter 5 you'll learn the key differences between two business models that will take you to Freedom, where trading your time for money will become optional. The two business models are the *Profit* Business and the *Legacy* Business.

Then, in PART II we're going to dive deep into how you create Financial Freedom for yourself through your business model. You'll learn *The 3 Phases of Financial Freedom:* **Crystalize, Customize and Monetize.**

These three phases will transform your business from the ground up, into one that builds your Freedom and allows you to make the greatest impact in the world. You'll especially love a little 'pricing secret' we'll outline in detail within the *Monetize Phase*. It basically enables you to find the perfect price for each of your products and services so that your business will inevitably take you to Freedom. Pricing is something that so many business owners (needlessly) struggle with. Few know they're are in unique position to not only become Free themselves but to share their gifts in a way to accelerate Freedom.

This book is something Tony and I are so proud of. It's the product of working with business owners over the years, all we know to create a massive rewiring of your mind around money plus practical strategies that build businesses to create Freedom. We've shared all we can to help you build freedom and be the person who makes the fullest impact they can. We are so thrilled you are here with us.

As you implement what you learn, you create a *new normal* for yourself. We need to reach approximately 20,000,000 people like you and every person counts. Every individual who implements this knowledge and creates Freedom in their life becomes like a beacon of light that lets other's know Freedom is possible for them.

YOU ROCK!

Makaylah Rogers
Co-Founder of MindShift.money

PART I
THE ULTIMATE
MINDSHIFT

CHAPTER 1

CRITICAL MINDSHIFTS AROUND MONEY

To most people, $147,000.00 sounds like a lot of money.

However, when you're 65 years old and that's all the money you have to survive on for the rest of your life: it doesn't seem like a lot at all. That scenario happens to the majority of people who (attempt to) retire at 65.

A recent survey, "Perspectives on Retirement by Generation," was conducted by transamericacenter.org. The survey showed the generation of baby boomers is entering retirement with only $147,000.00 median net worth to live off for the rest of there life (which is estimated to be another 20+ years!). That means if they stop working at 65; they have a whole $612.50 per month to support themselves if they wanted their retirement savings to last 20 years! Often that's not even enough to cover the cost of a mortgage or rent payment. Could you make that work for your current lifestyle?

We don't share such a bleak statistic to scare you. In fact, the opposite: we hope it opens your eyes to a reality you may be living right now, giving you the motivation to change your course and create something new.

Diagnosing Financial Sickness

As a doctor of medicine (Tony), I saw thousands of people who suffered from countless ailments. Each person was unique and, as a result, his or her treatment plan was unique. If a patient walked into our office with chest pain, I asked a series of questions to define where the pain was located and what type of pain it was.

Sometimes it turned out to be a minor problem: they had strained a muscle at the gym. Other times it was a serious problem like a heart attack or cancerous tumor in their lung. Either way, only after I knew what was causing their pain could I offer my best suggestion to treat it. Accurately diagnosing a health challenge is the first step to become healthy again.

I've noticed the same way your body needs a regular physical check-up, it's important to examine how well your financial health is. That way you can find out if you're financially sick, and then determine what's causing that sickness. That way, you can cure it forever.

In fact, the whole concept of financial wellness was the basis for my first book series called Financially Fit! That series outlined some of the fundamental principles anyone can use to take control of their money and become financially free.

In the second part of this book, you'll use some of those fundamental principles to grow your wealth (more on that later). We can't count the number of times we've spoken to business owners who appear successful on the outside, yet in reality, their finances show signs of near-death toxicity.

They drive a beautiful car. They live in a safe, upper-class neighborhood, in a large house. They wear high quality clothing and so does their family. Looking at them from the outside, they have everything that characterizes a *successful person*.

If you talk to most successful business owners for long enough and ask them questions about their finances, in less than ten minutes, if they'll answer honestly, it becomes clear:

- They aren't paying themselves a consistent income from their business (usually they work the hardest and are paid the least!);
- They're drenched in consumer and business debt and have no clue how they're going to dig themselves out;
- Their net worth isn't growing fast enough to support them and their family long term;

- They have little or zero buffer money if an unexpected bill arises;
- They do not have passive income that supports all their basic expenses;
- They are completely (secretly) stressed about money.

In other words, they're financially sick as hell. Plus, they feel so isolated. Others see them as successful and don't understand what they are going through. This makes it extremely difficult for an entrepreneur to allow themselves to be vulnerable enough to talk about their challenges. Instead, they put on their happy and successful mask to make everyone believe they're in good condition and life is just rosy for them. And they continue to keep up with the Jones's.

The Financially Sick Doctor

After being accepted into medical school, I remember thinking to myself, "Finally, I've made it! It's all smooth sailing from here on out!" Then I graduated and started my locum at a hospital in Perth, Australia. The novelty of graduating into such an esteemed profession quickly wore out.

The picture in my head transformed from: "life as a respected doctor, with green lights down every boulevard, and a beds made of rose petals" into my new reality, which looked more like: "a stressed-out, sleep-deprived, workaholic... Who just happened to wear a white lab coat and have a higher than average salary." The eighty-hour workweeks began wearing me down. A feeling of constant exhaustion – like a cloud over my head that wouldn't stop raining – became normal. I took my stress home with me, my enjoyment of life evaporated, and my health started to suffer. Often – even though I was physically exhausted – at night, I couldn't fall asleep because my mind would race with things I had to do the next day. The mayhem continued day in and day out.

Also, the doctors, registrars, and consultants I worked amongst seemed completely stressed out too. They spent little time with their families, and didn't appear to gain fulfillment from their work. It looked like the more time they spent working, the more miserable they became. It's ironic, but you'd be surprised by the amount of doctors who take up smoking. They do this to cope with the amount of stress they feel.

Each year, the winter came around, and like clockwork, these doctors took an expensive two-week vacation. Regardless of where they were going, and what they'd do when they got there, vacation was their best attempt to make up for lost time with their family. These men and women felt guilty for neglecting their family so they tried to make up for it by buying their family expensive gifts.

As a father of two boys, nothing is more painful than looking into your child's eyes after missing something that was is important to them and saying, "Sorry I couldn't be there son, daddy had to work." Each time that happens, they become a little more distant and mistrusting of whether they are really as important to you as you say they are.

In addition, as a general rule, my peers worked until the day they died. I used to think wow, these people must love their jobs so much: they just keep working until they're in their 60's and 70's!

But the reality was: financially, my coworkers couldn't stop working. They needed to work in order to cover their monthly expenses. And we're told in school being a doctor is an "aspiration career". It wasn't long before I started to second-guess the "glorious" profession I'd chosen. Then one night, I experienced a defining moment of absolute clarity...

... While sitting in my kitchen in Perth, two questions emerged in my mind that motivated me to gain control of my finances and become financially free once and for all. I asked myself the first question: "If something happened right now that caused me to be unable to work, how long would my money last?"

Then the next question arose in my mind: "Do I really want to live a life where I must work in order for money to come in?" At first, asking these questions frightened me because they revealed how exposed I was financially. If anything bad were to happen that disabled me from going to work and earning money, it would have placed an enormous stress on my family. That was unacceptable.

So I then asked myself: Could there be a way for me to pay for my basic living expenses that doesn't require my time? At that moment in time, if I stopped working, my money would run out within four months. Plus, I had no way of making money that didn't require my time. The reality I faced that night in the kitchen was similar to the majority of people who live in developed countries. So, next we're going to uncover the reason such financial stress exists for the majority of people.

What is the cause?

The Cause of Financial Sickness

354.06 million people live in North America. On average, they live are now living past eighty years of age, and this is increasing (it is projected that 2 out of every three children born today will live past 100!). At the end of their working life, after 40+ years of working, ninety-six out of 100 of these people, don't have enough money to independently support themselves. In fact, the overwhelming majority require financial assistance from the government and family. Based on those statistics, there is a better than 96% chance that if you stopped working now, your money would probably last you less than a couple years, and I'm guessing that it would be much less than that.

It's also likely that you do not have a mechanism that pays for your basic living expenses (without requiring your time to make it work). That is a big problem. It makes you highly vulnerable to having to exchange your time for money...and to have to remain healthy enough to do so! So, what causes this financial disparity in so many people?

Why is it out of every one hundred people, only four reach financial freedom, while the other ninety-six fail? Similar to diagnosing the cause of a health challenge, there isn't a single, one-size-fits-all answer to that question. We can, however, define the main causes and then learn the process to remedy each one so they no longer plague us.

There are three main causes of financial sickness:

- Your Wealth Mindset: the subjective vision of yourself and the world around you.
- Real-World Issues: the factual realities of the world that are out of your control, yet affect your money.

- No Clear Destination: the lack of a clear goal to become financially free; and a plan to progressively reduce your reliance on exchanging your time for money along the way to this goal.

The more aware you are of these: the better you become at manifesting your dreams. You will never arrive at a destination that you never decide to travel to (Financial Freedom in this case). Equally, without a congruent mindset toward financial freedom, you won't achieve it, and without an awareness of the real-world issues surrounding finances, you leave yourself (and your family) in a vulnerable position, both short-term and long-term.

We'll explore mindset first; then go into the real world issues surrounding money in the next chapter; before spending the remainder of the book on achieving financial freedom and specifically – how to use your business to accelerate to personal financial freedom.

Sound good?

The Money Myths That Keep People Trapped

How you use your mind determines the results you'll produce in the physical world. If you have a mindset that tells you you're bad at investing or managing your money, it's likely you will not do it. It's that simple.

If you have a mindset that tells you you're good at investing and money management, when you do it: you'll probably succeed. Success truly is how you set your mind.

Before we move on, let's address a potential elephant in the room that could prevent you from getting the most out of the next few pages.

We are exposed to so much personal development material that covers the topic of mindset that it's easy to roll your eyes when you hear it again. People automatically say, "Yeah, mindset, I know, I know... In order to succeed, I've got to have the right mindset... yeah I got it! Let's get to the How-To Information"

One of the worst things you can do to your mind is shut it off. The topic of mindset is the most mission-critical element to your success. Hands down, bar none. As the great author Leo Buscaglia said: *"To know, and not to do, is not to know."* If

10

you're not getting the results you want in life – "financial freedom" being one of those results – your mindset is probably incongruent with your desires. So, it's important for you to re-examine your current mindset and make the tweaks necessary for you to succeed.

What follows is a breakdown of two of the most devastating money myths that prevent people from becoming financially free. Eliminate these mindsets and you're virtually guaranteed to win in business, in life and in money.

Money Myth #1:
Money Is Scarce

People who believe money is scarce in some way often communicate things like:
- "Money is hard to come by."
- "If I get rich, it's at the expense of others."
- "There isn't enough money to go around."
- "The rich get richer, while the poor get poorer."

Just as the sun rises in the East and sets in the West, misinformed people have been repeating these false beliefs, probably since money was first invented.

Most of us have heard these mindsets throughout our lives from our parents, grandparents, teachers, maybe even our financial advisors! This brainwashing is passed down from generation to generation. The net effect has created epic, global levels of debt and stress.

Why Money is Abundant and Never Scarce

During the Great Depression, there was a man named Michael J. Cullen, who worked as an employee for a grocery store called The Kroger Company.

During his time at work, Cullen thought of new, innovative ways to increase the company's efficiency and profit. The more he thought about his ideas, the more tangible they became, the greater his belief grew that they could become a reality.
As Napoleon Hill says, Cullen's thoughts turned into burning desires. One day, Cullen wrote a letter to the president of Kroger. In the letter, he proposed a business partnership and outlined the ways he could help grow the company.

He painted a picture of a new store that focused on advertising low prices; utilizing old factory space for storefront locations; eliminating delivery services; and offering cash sales to attract people into the store.

His letter did not receive a reply from the president of Kroger, yet by that time it didn't matter. Michael J. Cullen was so confident his idea would work; he quit his job, went out on his own, and started The King Kullen Grocery Store Chain.

The store offered benefits to the price-conscious shoppers of the Great Depression that were more attractive than the ones that existed previously. By 1936 there were seventeen locations with revenues of approximately $6,000,000.00 ($102,836,956.52 in 2016's currency).

The Most Abundant Resource Begins with "V." Money is nothing more than a measure of <u>value</u> you produce in the marketplace. The more value you produce, the more money you'll receive in exchange.

Michael J. Cullen's story illustrates how someone, in the most challenging economic conditions can increase their value and earn more money as a result. His story is one example of thousands who prospered in The Depression by developing new ways to support the market's wants.

In fact there are seven additional, "billion dollar reasons," why this myth is total, utter B.S. Before we look at each one, I want to share a quote with you from one of the founding fathers of the United States, Benjamin Franklin. Keep his words in mind as we move forward. *"I observed...the more public provisions were made for the poor, the less they provided for themselves, and of*

13

course became poorer. And, on the contrary, the less was done for them, the more they did for themselves, and became richer."

Billionaires Who Were Born Broke

Over the last century there have been tens of thousands of people who were born without many financial resources and became millionaires, multi-millionaires and billionaires in their lifetime. They did not have special privileges – they worked and created opportunities using the same two things you and I have too: a mind, and a will to succeed by providing value in the marketplace. The following is a list of five people, who were born into families of modest means and refused to believe money, opportunity, or success was limited and scarce. They all became billionaires in their lifetime.

You may not want to become a billionaire. Most people do not. The point of these stories is not to tell you what you should want. The purpose of these stories is to engage your mind about the opportunities you have to create the life you truly desire.

The First "Born Broke Billionaire"

After his single mother could not support John Paul Dejoria as a child: he lived in a foster home, and as he grew older, he lived out of his car. In 1980, he and hairdresser Paul Mitchell, started a company called John Paul Mitchell Systems. His net worth is

14

somewhere in the neighborhood of 2.8 billion dollars

The Second "Born Broke Billionaire"

From 60 to 16,000 outlet stores, Starbucks CEO, Howard Schultz, said: "Growing up I always felt like I was living on the other side of the tracks. I knew the people on the other side had more resources, more money, and happier families… "And for some reason, I don't know why or how, I wanted to climb over that fence and achieve something beyond what people were saying was possible. I may have a suit and tie on now but I know where I'm from and I know what it's like."

The Third "Born Broke Billionaire"

The all-time Queen of Media, Oprah Winfrey, was born into a poor family in Mississippi. She succeeded in becoming an AM talk show host in Chicago that later became, The Oprah Winfrey Show. Oprah once said: "I don't think of myself as a poor deprived ghetto girl who made good. I think of myself as somebody who, from an early age, knew I was responsible for myself, and I had to make good."

The Fourth "Born Broke Billionaire"

You probably aren't familiar with Frieda Cutler and Frank Lifshitz, are you? They were two Ashkenazi Jews who immigrated to the Bronx, New York City. Frieda was an artist and Frank was a house painter. I can almost guarantee you don't know of them

15

but you probably know their youngest son, Ralph Lauren. Ralph dropped out of college, worked at Brooks Brothers as a sales assistant, then left to become a salesman for a tie company. When he was 26 years old, he felt inspired to design a wide, European-style necktie but the company he worked for rejected the idea. They said it was, "not commercially viable." One year later Ralph started his own company, designed his own ties and sold them under the table, under the band name "Polo". By 2007 Ralph Lauren had over 35 boutiques in the United States. His approximate net worth is $5.5 billion dollars.

The Fifth "Born Broke Billionaire"

Hopefully by now you see the myth that "money is scarce" as a nonsensical notion. Wealth doesn't happen via luck, wishful thinking or using magic. However, writing about magic did bring about massive financial success for one woman. A financially stressed single mother with little resources had an idea that she needed to share with others. Before J.K. Rowling's Harry Potter series became a blockbuster success, she used to work in cafés because she didn't have an office to work from. Her publisher once said she should "find a day job." Instead she shared her story with the world and it fascinated millions of people, while providing her with a billion dollar net worth.

Focus on the value you can create: money will follow

Sometimes terms like: "The Marketplace," and, "The Economy," can have the tendency to sound as if they're singular things. Maybe it's because we hear them so often from newsrooms: "The economy isn't doing so well. There's a dip in the economy. New research on the economy shows..." It's easy for their true definition to get fogged up over time.

The marketplace and the economy are simply: a large collection of people who spend money. It's a constantly moving, changing relationship between groups of people who spend their money to get what they want. Each person in the economy has his or her own desires, wants, and needs they seek to fulfill. Each spends money to fulfill those desires. If it sounds to you as if we're belaboring the definition of "economy," It's for good reason. It's for you to understand this next fact at a deep level. If you'll grasp this next concept's potency, you will always have an abundance of money, regardless of what happens in your marketplace.

Here it is: since there are so many people in the economy and those people's wants, needs and desires are virtually limitless... SO IS MONEY! Remember, the most abundant resource on Earth is people's desires for value. It is never scarce. People's desires are always expanding. Whether a person is bored and wants a new exciting experience, or they're cold and want to feel comfortable again: one moment they have a problem and the next moment they find a solution. Between each problem and its solution is an exchange of something. That's where you can choose to come in. Think of how to solve people's problems. Solve enough people's problems, and money will not be a problem for you ever again.

If you want to earn more money, you need to take time to find out how to serve the needs and wants of the people who make up your marketplace. Become a problem-seeking bloodhound who sniffs around for ways to add more value to people's lives. The men and women who believe money is scarce are not thinking of enough new, innovative ways to benefit The People.

Scarcity of money is not the problem:
their scarceness of thought is.

Remember: the amount of money you earn is in direct proportion to the amount of value you provide the people in your marketplace. Since people's desire to gain value is infinite: so is money. If the feelings of scarcity creep up on you, take some time and write down ways you could help people solve their problems. Also, revisit our list of five billionaires mentioned in this chapter, search on Google and read their biographies. Allow their story to inspire you to new heights. You are designed to accomplish greater levels of financial wellbeing just as they did. You are more similar to them than you are different.

Money Myth #2:
More Money Is Unethical

Common phrases that misinformed people say in regard to the ethics of money are:

- "Money is the root of all evil."
- "In order to get rich, I need to manipulate people."
- "Wealthy people sacrifice happiness for money."

If there were one money myth we could snap our fingers and get the World to leave behind, it would be: "Money is the root of all evil." Where did this stupid idea come from and why would anyone choose to believe that? Our team was attending a conference about a year ago and there were two women having a conversation in the hotel lobby. They were talking about how money relates to politics.

The one woman said, "Well, it all comes down to money... No one cares about anything else." Her friend agreed, "Yep, it even says it in the Bible, 'Money is the root of all evil.'"
We searched: "Where in the Bible does it say 'Money is the root of all evil?'" Our assumption the woman took the quote out of context was correct. What the passage really says is: **"For the love of money is the root of all kinds of evil - Timothy 6:10."** As you can see, the subject of the passage addresses the love of money being the root of evil. It doesn't say that

money itself is the root of evil. Have you ever purchased something and gained a benefit from it? Meaning, as a result of the purchase you made you solved a problem, or you had a great time, or something good came from it? Maybe you bought a plane ticket and went on a vacation to a country you'd never visited before. Perhaps you bought a gift for someone's birthday; or you went to a movie with your children; or you purchased lunch for yourself and a friend. Whatever you bought, you did it with money. IF money is the root of all evil, THEN are those experiences evil, too?

- Is a child's bicycle helmet evil?
- Is the food you eat for breakfast evil?
- Are a pair of shoes or sandals evil?
- Is the money you give to charity evil?

Name any thing. A university building; a public transit system; a painted, hand woven basket; a pair of tickets to a sporting event; whatever you can think of. Are any of those things evil?
Of course they aren't, yet all of them are gained in exchange for money. I'd also suggest that none of those things I mentioned – money included – are "the root of all good" either. They are just things. Those things are either value to us, or they're not, but to call them good or evil is simply inaccurate and a waste of energy. Money is only a tool for amplifying who we really are.

You can use that tool for good or for evil. If you're a kind person, you can amplify your kindness by using your money to help people. If you're an evil person, you can amplify your evilness by using money to harm people. The choice is in your hands.

The Definition of Success

There are many people who distort the ethics of money. They think success comes at the cost of being morally questionable. If you have money, it means you did something that wasn't completely honest to get it. So, let's take a look at why this mindset is untrue and worth removing from your mind forever. In 1956, there was a man named, Earl Nightingale, who recorded an album called The Strangest Secret. The album sold over a million copies and it became the first spoken-word recording to achieve Gold status.

In The Strangest Secret, Earl Nightingale defines the word SUCCESS as: "**A progressive realization of a worthy ideal**" He said that if you are progressively realizing a worthy ideal, money will flow in abundance.

One of the key words in that definition is: worthy. If you want to get wealthy by trafficking drugs, or becoming a professional thief, or a contract killer, those are certainly not worthy ideals. They are professions that steal value from the marketplace and do more harm than good. You may earn a lot of money doing

21

those things, but the money you earn is worth less. It will still buy you the same stuff that ordinary money can, but it comes with an invisible tax. Every time you earn more, a little chunk of happiness gets taken away from you. Your soul gets diluted with every dollar you earn. Not to mention, you're likely to end up in jail (or a coffin) if you do them long enough. As we mentioned in Money Myth #1: "the amount of money you earn is in direct proportion to the amount of value you provide the people in your marketplace."

The more money you earn: the more you contribute to those around you. That means, as long as you're contributing real value in the marketplace it is absolutely ethical for you earn as much money as you want. Make sure your endeavors are worthy. Help people solve their problems and realize the money you earn is just a by-product of that service. Make your service to others your top priority and also know: the more you serve, the more money you make. Money always follows service. Remember this: If what you do contributes to people's lives, you deserve every dollar you earn

Money Myth #3:
The Most Dangerous Myth Of All

It was a real challenge to determine which money myths to share in this book and which ones to omit. There are over one-dozen myths and misconceptions we could've shared and broken down. For instance:

- "I am financially secure because I've got a job."
- "My bank has my best interest at heart."
- "Having a home mortgage is a good investment."
- "Student loans are 'good debt'."
- "I'm wealthy because I earn a lot of money."
- "I need to be on a budget to build wealth."
- "I should get out of debt, then start investing."

All of those myths inhibit our ability to become financially free in the fastest amount of time. However, we're not going to address those now because you'll overcome those mindsets indirectly, as you continue to read. (To find out more about some of the Money Myths mentioned above go to MindShift.money). The Money Myth we are choosing to share in this last part is the most debilitating, and freedom-stealing myth of all. If the "money-is-scarce myth," and the, "money-is-unethical myth," got together and gave birth to an evil child, that child would be the myth I am about to reveal. It is responsible for millions upon millions of hardworking people who live their whole life, yet will never become financially. Here it is:

"Go to _____, get good _____,
get a secure _____. Time equals _____."

You'll notice we left out four words from the sentence, yet you probably didn't have any trouble filling in the blanks. Of the people we share that exercise with, nine out of ten fill in those blanks with the exact same words as the other people. With robotic consistency, the majority of people write, "Go to school, get good grades, get a secure job, save your money, and time equals money."

Before we move on... We realize you run a business; you don't technically have a "job". However, of the 28 million small businesses that are registered in the US, 26 million of them have less than 3 employees. That means to most business owners: their business is their job and they are their boss. Another way of saying it is they still exchange their time for money. If they are not physically present at work, things begin to fall apart and their income declines... From now on, instead of 'job,' we'll say 'they exchange their time for money' so we can maintain consistency throughout this book. There are three reasons why the myth, "Go to school, get good grades, and go exchange your time for money," is an <u>especially dangerous</u> myth:

1. It's actually multiple myths wrapped into one phrase.
2. The advice may have worked at one time, but is no longer applicable in today's society.
3. So many people share this exact same belief!

In other words, multiple parts of this myth are completely false, and don't work in today's society, yet so many people unconsciously accept it is true, never question it, and act in accordance to their beliefs. In the next chapter, "The Matrix of Money," we will give you a list of facts that support why this myth is false. It goes all the way back to Industrial Age Thinking; it's the type of mindset that is based in the past and in today's world, holds us back severely. Before you flip to the second chapter, however, we're going to breakdown the #1 reason WHY these Money Myth exists and why they are prevalent in the mindsets of so many people.

Who's Time Are You On?

There's a story of a well-dressed man who walks in front of a watchmakers store every morning on his way to work. Each morning as he walks past the store, he peers in at the large wooden clock that rests in the glass display case. He then sets the time on his wristwatch to the clock and keeps walking to work. The man follows that same ritual morning after morning, for years. One day, as he approaches the store, he notices the watchmaker is standing outside sweeping the sidewalk. The well-dressed man gives a friendly nod to the watchmaker. The watchmaker looks over and says... "Hi there. You know, I've owned this shop for about twenty years, and I couldn't help but notice you stop here every morning and set your wristwatch to my big clock here in the display. What is it that you need to keep such close time for?" The well dressed man replies; "Indeed, I've stopped here every day for a whole twenty years. It sure is funny how time flies... I'm one of the two foremen at the power plant down the road. Among other tasks, I'm in charge of letting our staff know when their breaks are, and I also sound the end-of-day whistle at 5PM."

"Well isn't that the darndest thing..." The watchmaker says in a puzzled way. "You know... For all these years I've set my clock's time to the sound of power plant's whistle!"

#Don't Be a Sheep

If a stranger tapped on your shoulder in your local coffee shop, looked at you and said, "Sit! Lie down! Stay! Roll over!" Would you do it? Of course not, right? So, why do such large groups of people obey general society's orders to, "Go to school, get good grades, and go exchange their precious time for money," and, like sheep, unquestioningly follow the others in a group? Why are most people like the watchmaker and the well-dressed man who – despite being hard working, educated, and skilled – still act without any critical thought of what they're doing?

The answer is simple: it's human nature.

In an article by the Harvard Business Review there was a quote that said, "You can take the person out of the Stone Age, but can't take the Stone Age out of the person." It appears as though we live in a sophisticated environment full of technology aiming to make our lives efficient and comfortable. Our quality of life is exponentially better than our Stone Age ancestors' lives were; yet our psychology hasn't changed much, if at all.

In his book, The War of Art, Steven Pressfield shares an insight about why people blindly follow one another. He says: "We run naturally in packs and cliques; without thinking about it, we know who's the top dog and who's the underdog. And we know our own place. We define ourselves, instinctively it seems, by our position within the schoolyard, the gang, the club."

Earl Nightingale also touched on human's natural sheep-like behavior in his album I mentioned earlier, The Strangest Secret: "Rollo May, the distinguished psychiatrist, wrote a wonderful book called Man's Search for Himself, and in this book he says: 'the opposite of courage in our society is not cowardice... It is conformity.' And there you have the reason for so many failures! Conformity and people acting like everyone else, without knowing why they are doing it or where they are going. We learn to read by the time we're seven. We learn to make a living by the time we're 30. Often by that time we're not only making a living, we're supporting a family. And, yet, by the time we're 65, we haven't learned how to become financially independent in the wealthiest countries at some of the wealthiest times that have ever been known. Why? We conform!"

You may think, "Well, I don't conform. I'm an entrepreneur damn it! I think for myself always. How other people act doesn't control me." Are you really sure? Even the world's most intelligent scientists and rocket engineers are just as susceptible to the magnetic tides of conformity as you and we are. In one case, a certain strain of conformity took the lives of seven astronauts.

The Death of Conformity

While traveling in Florida with my (Tony) wife and kids, we took a trip out to the Kennedy Space Center. It was awe-inspiring and we found ourselves behind a tour group, led by a professor. The professor talked about the different areas of their Program. He also told us a story about the 28th mission of the Columbia space shuttle. This was it's devastating last mission...the one where Columbia burnt up on re-entry to the atmosphere, killing all seven crewmembers on board.

It was terribly sad to hear the story. At the same time it was fascinating because the mind set behind the circumstances that caused the incident is the root cause of so many of the serious problems that exist around us. In the investigation after the accident, it was determined that a large piece of foam fell off one of the shuttle's fuel tanks and damaged the wing of the spacecraft. The investigation also revealed the people in charge of the project at NASA were aware of the problem while they conducted previous test flights.

"So, why did NASA choose to send the rocket into space, if they knew such a problem existed?" The professor asked the group in our tour. "The answer is: Normalization of deviance." He then told us about Diane Vaughan, a sociologist and author, who defined normalization of deviance in her book: The Challenger Launch Decision. She defined it as: "The gradual process through which unacceptable practice or standards become acceptable. As the deviant behavior is repeated without catastrophic results, it becomes the social norm for the organization."

The professor said before the tragedy happened, the people working on The Columbia Mission spoke about re-positioning the military satellites to look underneath the space shuttle for flaws. They spoke about doing a space walk to have access and look at the damage. They spoke of a number of things, but acted on none of them and their error ended up costing seven people's lives. Conformity can literally kill.

The Counter-Intuitive Art of Winning

During this chapter we deconstructed three Money Myths; negative mindsets that prevent the majority of people from achieving the dreams they deserve to create. To summarize:

1. Money is not scarce, it's abundant.
2. Money is ethical if it's acquired by creating value.
3. "Go to school, get good grades, and go exchange your precious time for money," is an outdated mindset from the industrial revolution.

The final and most significant concept to grasp about these myths is to understand why they spread. The reason they spread from one person to another is because we conform. Success is a counter-intuitive process. It's human nature to want expediency over patience. It's our nature to want answers given to us rather than figuring them out ourselves.

It takes guts to overcome our automatic human responses. As we break through our autopilot, thoughtless nature, we enjoy new levels of success and satisfaction. You'll notice as you read on, the purpose of this book is: "To help you become conscious of the moves you make in your business/personal worlds that impact your world, and direct those actions to become Financially Free. Being a business owner, this means you then also maximize your impact in the world as a result."

30

By becoming conscious of your actions, you're taking the first step to overcome conformity and create those counter-intuitive action habits the financially free 4% of the world have that others do not. Thinking and acting by your own design isn't just to create financial freedom, it's the only way to be truly free.

In the next chapter we will review some real world facts that influence your money and your freedom. This next chapter is epic, a true game changer. Read carefully because the insights you'll gain will help you avoid the traps that so many are unconsciously headed for.

CHAPTER #2

THE MATRIX OF MONEY

When we first saw the movie The Matrix, starring Keanu Reeves and Laurence Fishburne, we looked at each other and said, "Isn't this perfect! What a great metaphor for the world of finances."

In the movie, a computer hacker named Neo (Reeves) discovers the world he lives in is actually a simulated reality called "the Matrix." He meets a man named Morpheus (Fishburne) who gives Neo the opportunity to awaken from the Matrix into the real world by swallowing a red pill.

When Neo wakes up, the real world is an apocalyptic desert land, where robots called Sentinels harvest human body heat for energy. The Sentinels created the simulated reality of The Matrix to keep the human's minds distracted, preventing them from starting a revolution against their robot tyranny.

Morpheus is the leader of a group of rebels who hack into the Matrix to awaken humans like Neo from their bondage. The rebels understand how the Matrix really works. When they hack into it, they can bend its physical laws and do cool, superhuman stuff. For instance, they can dodge bullets and jump across massive gaps between skyscrapers. It's pretty damn awesome!

There's a scene near the end of the movie where Neo reaches an enlightened state of being. A group of enemies shoot their guns at Neo and everything slows down. Neo puts his hand up and stops the bullets in mid air.

Then he looks around and everything he sees – the walls, the floor, the guns, his enemies – transform into binary code (a type computer programming made off 1's and 0's). He manipulates the binary code with his mind and is finally able to destroy his enemies. The end.

If you consider it for a moment:
most people live in their own Matrix.

We're not saying we live in a simulated reality, governed by Sentinel robots that harvest our body heat. What we mean is most people live their life as slaves to the norm. They end up following what everyone else is doing just because it's what everyone does. The majority of people run their life and finances based on habits and ways of doing things that are normal in our society because they lack awareness and knowledge that says it should be done differently.

33

There's a problem with this Money Matrix. A huge one. And it is our intention to wake you up to the problem like Neo and Morpheous did in The Matrix.

In order to see the matrix of money, you must have a basic understanding of key things that have happened in the history of money and the concerning place we are left in at this point in time. In understanding this, you will see through the matrix of money and be empower yourself to break free. We will keep this as brief as possible, outlining only the essentials. History is often thought of as a boring subject but understanding these few parts of our financial history will likely empower you to create Freedom like nothing else.

As you read the following section that gives you the key historical elements to be aware of, keep these words of wisdom in mind... Sir Winston Churchill, the British politician and Nobel Prize winning author once said: "The farther back you can look, the farther forward you are likely to see." And the philosopher and novelists, George Santayana, said: "Those who do not remember the past are condemned to repeat it." Let's be inspired to create a different financial future by understanding what's happened in the past.

The Financial Perfect Storm

Around 1870, there was a second wave of the industrial revolution that begun. The economy was growing at a rapid rate and jobs were abundant. There was a need for both skilled and unskilled laborers in the workforce. In 1875 the American Express Company designed the first private pension plan in the United States. This was the first time a company had taken responsibility for supporting employees after their working life. By 1919 over 300 pension plans existed. Large companies, States and the Federal Government began to use pensions as a way to attract employees to come work for them.

The people in Big Business looked at pensions as a good deal because the average life expectancy was between 50 and 53 for men and women. Therefore companies usually didn't have to pay for pensions when a person retired because they often died before that time.

The first pension plans were called defined pension plans. These plans were set up in such a way that when the employee retires, the company was obligated to pay a defined amount, often two-thirds of the average of their previous salary, until they the retiree dies. Then when the retiree passed away they would continue at 50% to your surviving spouse.

Fast-forward almost 150 years from the first pension plan and the average lifespan is now between 80 and 83 for men and women! Plus two out of every three of kids born today will live beyond 100! This wasn't the case when pension plans were first created. There has been a massive change in longevity. This increase in longevity has significant financial impact.

Let's explore this...

If you're expecting to retire at 65 but are going to live another 25 years of nonworking life, how does that affect your money? Defined pension plans worked well when employees only lived for three years after they left the company, but not okay when 3 years became 25 years. Increased longevity placed massive pressure on governments and corporations. This is one of the things that caused the downfall of Detroit. Around the mid-80s, America introduced the ERISA legislation to handle this growing crisis. ERISA took us off defined benefit pension schemes and moved us to defined contribution pension schemes. That was the same advent of the RSPs in Canada, the superannuation system here in Australia, and 401Ks and the Roths in the United States.

These were plans were marketed to the public as a benefit to the employees. It was marketed in a way to make them think the companies were taking care of them in their retirement. The

36

goal wasn't to set them up for retirement; the goal was to get them off the pension because it was bankrupting state governments and big corporations.

Okay here is where sh*t is about to get real crazy. This is where the real passion for our movement comes from. By moving away from the old defined pension plan, government and corporations were no longer responsible for employees at the end of their working life. This means that from this point forward, the responsibility for taking care of ourselves when we can no longer work fell on the employees. Here's the problem with that. It's massive. Stay with me here because this all links back to you as a business owner. So the responsibility for taking care of themselves now falls on the employees. This has led to two severe problems:

1. Employees had now become investors. The employees were now responsible for the investments that fund themselves after working life. Now no one let people know that they now had become investors. On top of that there was also no education around how to invest. As you can imagine, the world of investments is complex and the vast majority of the population has no knowledge of how to invest. So here we now have a large population that is financially illiterate and now responsible for the investments that fund their retirement.

This is a big problem. This problem is compounded when we look at the second severe problem:

2. The vast majority of employees don't know how much money they need to support themselves once they stop working. Up to this point in time, employees were used to the idea they would have a pension – that the government or their employer would take care of them. They were used to the idea that they would be okay after their working life because up to that point the company paid two-thirds of their salary until the day they died. They were used to the expectation of being taken care of. This was no longer the case after ERISA. Now the employee must know how much to invest in order to have enough money for their basic needs once they stop working. Once again, there was no education on this. So the vast majority of the population is ending their working life with nowhere near enough money to live on.

The general population is therefore, financially illiterate, is living longer than ever before and thinks that there is money set up to last them into perpetuity because they're used to the idea that they will be taken care of. In actual fact it was only set up as short-term measures to veer people off the pension leaving them responsible for funding themselves at the end of their working life, with no knowledge on how to do that properly.

Now here's the scariest part. This is the reality for an employee. The statistic is that business owners are 50% worse off than employees at the end of their working life. We share this with you not to scare you but to light a fire inside of you to become empowered around your own finances. To treat this problem with the true energy and focus it needs in order to turn this around for you.

The next big challenge on the horizon has to do with the baby boomers. Baby boomers are the cohort born between 1946 and 1964, an 18-year cohort and one of the single biggest population bubbles that make up the biggest proportion of our population as a percentage. This cohort has impacted all the major trends we've seen including the growth in stock markets and the drivers behind it. The baby boomer generation started retiring around 2012 and thus exiting the work force and not paying taxes. So as more baby boomers retire there is less money for the government to use.

In addition, they're starting to withdraw from their pension schemes and our retirement savings accounts overall are starting to go down in size as an entire cohort. More people are withdrawing money from their pensions than new workers are putting money in, there are more people selling shares than buying shares and there are more people selling properties than buying properties. That means the supply and demand equation that has driven growth since the end of World War II is gone. How will growth occur if more people are trying to sell than buy? Much of what was held in the past doesn't hold true anymore. Now the first cohorts of baby boomers are starting to turn 72 in 2017. Statistically, that is when the average person starts needing extra support in their aged years: meal preparation, home care, home support, gardening support, and nursing and medical care. We're about to see a massive increase in healthcare costs like we've never seen; starting from next 2018 and it will last for at least 18 years.

Coming through a global financial crisis, almost all of the governments became bankrupt or at least heavily in debt. Costs are increasing while revenue is dropping. But the average family is raising 1.7 kids, a decline in family size means there are less workers to replace all of the people who are leaving the work force. This is a tricky catch 22 because the problem is a big one and the solution for it has to be long term. Government is less inclined to instigate changes that might cause short-term discomforts to create a long term solution for fear of votes going to the opposition who promise more appealing short term benefits rather than longer term solutions that have short term discomfort. Banks are driven by profit attained from selling debt so they have no interest in providing long-term solutions for the community unless it impacts on profitability.

So, do all these financial facts equal checkmate for us? Fortunately, no, these financial facts do not equal checkmate, especially for the people who educate themselves, like you're doing now. Is it really possible to become Financial Free in the midst of our "perfect storm of economic insanity"? The answer is of course! Yes, it is possible... And you as a business owner have a unique advantage if you pay close attention to the following chapters.

The Chet Holmes Story

In 2007, sales genius, Chet Holmes, wrote a New York Times best-selling book called, "The Ultimate Sales Machine." In the book, Chet describes a certain mindset business owners need to develop in regard to selling their products and services. He called this mindset, "pigheaded discipline and determination."

Basically, pigheaded discipline and determination is as it sounds. It's your capability to complete important tasks in your business and life. Without this skill, you're like a ship without a rudder, stuck in the middle of the ocean, on a windy night. You blow around from one aimless place to another. Instead of being at cause, you're at effect to the changing winds and tides. With pigheaded discipline and determination, you're like the Captain, who takes charge of the ship by opening the sails and motivating the crew to row the boat until you're safe at home.

Chet said, "The missing ingredient for nearly all of the 1,000-plus clients I have worked with directly to improve their businesses is pigheaded discipline and determination. We all get good ideas at seminars and from books, radio talk shows and business-building gurus. The problem is that most companies do not know how to identify and adapt the best ideas to their businesses.   Implementation, not ideas, is the key to real success."

You'll probably agree after seeing the problem that has been created throughout our financial history, your Freedom is an underline important task to complete. It's really, "The," important task to complete if you want to not only ensure you are taken care of at the end of your working life as well as fully express your gifts and talents in this lifetime.   The question you need to ask yourself is this: how willing are you to demonstrate Pig-Headed Discipline and Determination long enough to complete the task of YOUR Financial Freedom? On a scale of 1 – 10, how willing are you to persevere through the learning curve to create that in your life?

Pig-Headed Discipline and Determination in Action
Every single person I (Tony) have interacted with who is Financially Free needed to offset his or her short-term gratification in the name of what's really important.
There were moments on my journey I struggled with my own

desire to buy something expensive. For instance, I could afford to pay cash for an expensive car, but by making that purchase, I would delay the date I'd be Financially Free. It wasn't easy being at the car dealership, sitting behind the wheel of something that could go zero-to-sixty in less than five seconds, and then get out from behind that wheel and walk away (especially when you can afford it).

It wasn't always easy, and I didn't always make the right choices. But, the moments when I did made the right decision required pigheaded discipline and determination in order for me to make the decision that was in alignment with my objectives. What was the alternative? I suppose I could have lived my whole life, sick and tired of working in my business as a glorified employee, and time-slave. I could have remained as someone who, like 96% of the population, earned just enough money to wake up the next day and do it all over again, into infinitum. And end up like most business owners, 50% worse off than employees at the end of my working life. Yuck!

That was not an option for me. The thought of seeing my children as grown-ups, but not have the recollection of them growing, made me feel ill. And the thought of being without financial security was not okay with me. I wanted my Freedom like I needed my next breath!

I realized Freedom was not an option – it wasn't something nice to dream about – Freedom became a necessity. It became a MUST HAVE, and then it became a MUST HAVE, ASAP.

Just as the phrase suggests: "ask and it shall be given," once I seriously committed to create Financial Freedom in my life, resources, people, and ideas started to show up. In less than a two-year period of time, I built myself a Freedom Generator, (a concept you'll learn in this book) escaped from the time-for-money paradigm and ensured I was taken care of financially and no longer at risk of not being able to take care of my family and myself. Finally, I could leave medicine to follow my passions and money came in regardless if I went to "work" or not.

Based on over 25-years experience in the business world, and interacting with thousands of entrepreneurs, I've come to realize the ability to achieve Financial Freedom is not a talent; it's a learned skill-set and accessibility to the right information. Just as you can learn the skill of golf, or chess, or crossword puzzles, you can learn Financial Freedom.

I believe you and I are more similar than we are different from one another. If I learned and applied the knowledge I teach in this book, you can too. You can create Freedom for yourself, in fact, anyone can. The only thing that separates you from achieving Financial Freedom is your level of commitment.

If you will, as Chet Holmes said – apply pigheaded discipline and determination to becoming Financially Free – there is nothing that can stop you from achieving that. It's not the economy that determines your success: it's YOUR ECONOMY.

In the next chapter you're going to uncover what Freedom looks like for you. This is a mission critical step that we will build upon later in the book.

CHAPTER #3

WHAT FREEDOM IS TO <u>YOU</u>

When you started your business, did you do it as an expression of one of your personal gifts and talents? For instance, you're skilled at writing so you decided to offer copywriting services, or you love graphic design so you started a design business. Maybe you love helping people become clear on their business objectives so you started a coaching practice.

Whether your business is product or services based, you started it because at some level the benefits you provide are an expression of your Self. You're in business because it means something more than just money. You have a gift or a talent that you want to share in the marketplace. Also, when you started your business did you think about the impact you could create with your gift or talent? You feel it is your duty to offer service because when people buy from you, they gain genuine advantage over the other options they could have chosen from. Correct?

However, have you ever felt that you could be making a far greater impact in the world than you are right now? That there is more for you to express, more opportunities your business could expand into, yet something is still in the way, preventing you from creating that bigger impact?

The truth is: your gifts and impact can never fully take flight while you're personally financially dependent on your business. The average business owner has half of the personal wealth when compared to an equivalent person who's just stayed in a salary job. Only half of the personal wealth!

At the end of their useful working life, 80 percent of business owners end up closing their doors without drawing enough money from the business along the way to create their own Financial Freedom or setting up the business in a way that it can sell for enough to fund their Financial Freedom. Most business owners invest everything they've got into their business: time, effort and energy. They put so much into their work, yet end up 50% worse off than those who are employed. Why does that happen?

The fundamental reason a business owner's impact in the world doesn't have a chance to take full flight is because their business and personal worlds are financially intertwined. If their business catches a bit of a cold, so does their personal life. If they have financial needs in their personal life, they go to their business to withdraw funds. They have a constant expectation their business will cover their living expenses. That constant expectation creates an uncertainty in both worlds. Uncertainty results in hesitation, and with uncertainty you don't accurately plan your future. It's like placing their car's brakes on while expecting to move forward. Lastly, with uncertainty you get stress in the present moment and lack a clear pathway to move forward and do what's best for the business.

So, how does your business support the impact you want to create, while also providing for your personal financial needs now? In addition, how does your business secure your personal Financial Freedom?

In many cases, your impact will be reduced by your need for financial security from the business. You end up compromising your desire for larger impact to support your basic needs now. The ultimate way to stop contamination between your business world and your personal world is to create Freedom separate from your business. So, let's define what Freedom actually looks like for you.

The 3 Types of Freedom

When you hear the phrase: "Freedom doesn't live within your business. Freedom lives outside of your business," It may sound a little strange and paradoxical, because you probably started your business thinking it would provide you with the Freedom to spend your time in whatever way you'd like. If you started your business for Freedom, you're not alone.

The truth is that your business is actually meant to be a transition pathway to Freedom. Your business is the fuel you use to launch the rocket of Freedom in your life.

There are three, distinct types of Freedom.

Freedom # 1: Freedom of Choice

If you'll consider the underlying reason you desire Financial Freedom, it's because you want to choose how you spend your time in a state of pure desire, without compromise of any form.

Imagine the following...
Last night you called five of your friends to go out for dinner with you. The restaurant was world-class and your friend's company was too. When you ordered dinner, you only looked at the left side of the menu and chose whatever you wanted (without thinking of price). At the end of dinner, you picked up the bill and thought nothing of it.

Your friends and you started having a real good time, laughing and telling hilarious stories. The night was so fun, you felt like staying out longer than usual. By the time you got to bed, it was so late you could see the sun starting to light up the night's sky. When you woke up in the late morning, you still felt tired so you CHOSE to go back to bed and sleep until the afternoon. On a scale of 1 – 10 how "totally awesome" would it be, if that were your life? Not necessarily the specific example but generally. What if you could be the person who wakes up when you feel and does what you want, with whom you want to, simply because the choice is yours?

People want to be able to live a life of abundance. We want to live on our terms. We can work hard if we want to, and can take time off if we want to. Truly Freedom-based entrepreneurs – the ones who make it their top priority to achieve Freedom and form everything in their life around that outcome – create, "because I desire to" lifestyles and everyone creates "because I have to" lifestyles.

Truly Freedom based entrepreneurs, who become Financially Free outside their business, can be passionate about a cause and then if it no longer inspires them, they can drop it whenever they want. They are all in and smile and enjoy every moment because their mission inspires them. But when their desire with that mission begins to fade and it no longer interests them, they can get up and walk away without the slightest hesitation.

They want to – without apology, excuse or explanation – be able to open a new chapter, to start a new adventure in their life. They never get 'stale'. They want to drink from the nectar of life, completely soaked in their own moment-by-moment fascinations and interests. Ultimately isn't everybody searching for Freedom of Choice?

In order to create a "because I desire to" lifestyle, and finally have true Freedom of Choice, it is mission critical you break the link between time and money

Freedom #2: Financial Freedom

Around 2007 a large wave of companies, one-after-another, hopped on the "We're going green!" bandwagon. It was like a Going Green Gas Bomb exploded worldwide and the fumes took over every CMO's (Chief Marketing Officer's) mind at one time. Suddenly "green" was the new black.

The new advertising sounded as though the companies were taking positive actions toward creating a biologically sustainable planet. Some were, however most were conduced business as usual and did little or nothing to help the environment at all.

After a while, environmental activists came up with the term, "Green-Washing," to call BS on these companies, and bring awareness to the marketplace to make more (truly) conscious buying decisions. It wasn't long before, "We're going green!" became a limp term to shrug your shoulders at and say, "who cares?" in response to.

In the same way, the term, "Become Financially Free!" has become a term that has lost its potency through over-exposure. We've heard it so many times and often the images associated with it are bloated exaggerations of what Financial Freedom really is, and looks like in real life.

The "Beyoncé" Wealth Misconception

A lot of people talk about Financial Freedom. We hear about it as if it's living like Beyoncé, Brad Pitt, or any of the über successful stars. They make it look like Financial Freedom is you, traveling around in first class, drinking champagne all the time.

That is the biggest misconception about the topic of Financial Freedom; that it's a superstar life-style. Believing Financial Freedom is a grandiose; movie star lifestyle is probably one of the reasons why so few achieve it. They're intimidated by the unrealistic vision and the actions required to create such a vision. So they end up compromising. Your Financial Freedom is not that super star life.

Financial Freedom is Just a Number

It's important to understand that Financial Freedom is nothing more than a single number. We call it, "Your Freedom Number." It's the amount of income you need in your bank account each month to cover your basic living expenses, without you exchanging your time for that money.

In other words, it's passive income that covers all your living expenses, so you don't have to cover those expenses using your time, energy and effort. Keep in mind too, We're not saying a grand lifestyle is not realistic for you to achieve. We're saying it's important to demystify what Financial Freedom actually is so you can achieve it in the most direct, simple way possible. When you clear up a misconception, and get a clear vision of an objective reality (rather than a subjective one): you make the solution simpler to achieve.

Calculate your Freedom Number

Your personal Freedom Number is very simple to calculate. You simply add up all your monthly expenses. Once you have that number: you know exactly the amount of passive income you have to generate to officially call yourself Free.

One word of caution: there is a difference between what your bills total up to at the end of the month and what your actual monthly expenses are. What we're saying is: if you add up all your bills, that number most likely isn't what you actually spend each month. Most people spend more than that number. The easiest way to find out your actual Freedom Number is to look at your last twelve months of bank statements. You'll see what all your bills are, plus you'll see where else you're spending money on a regular basis (and how much money you're spending on those items.

Your Freedom Number is <u>one of four numbers</u> you need to know before you can truly turn your business into an accelerator to your Freedom. In Part #2 of this book you'll learn The 3 Phases of Financial Freedom, which includes a list of instructions to calculate all four numbers. It's easy, you'll see.

Freedom #3: Time

For so many of us the story we've been told when we go through life is to "go to school, get good grades and to go get good job, trading our time for money". But often the people who taught us that were usually not free themselves. They taught us what they knew…that the only way to make money is to trade your time for it! But your objectives are different from theirs so you need to think a little differently than they did.

Time is the most precious resource you have. It's the only thing you can never, ever get back. Bill Gates, one of the wealthiest people in the world, can't buy yesterday back. The reason people want Financial Freedom is generally because they want their time back, so they have the Freedom to choose how they spend their time, instead of being directed by tasks they don't control. Let's take a moment now and define the mechanism that provides you with Freedom outside your business. It's called a Freedom Generator.

What is a Freedom Generator?

Let's start by telling you what a Freedom Generator is not. A Freedom Generator is not a collection of 'get rich quick,' overnight, sketchy investments. Neither is it a portfolio full of risky investments. It is not stock trading; it's not developing real estate properties, its not building other businesses that require your time. A freedom generator is a collection of investments that are conservative, quality, and generate positive cash flow. Every month or quarter, you get paid from these investments, and they are not as subject to market volatility because they're more evergreen in the marketplace. Meaning, people will always need and want the services that back these investments up. Without you exchanging your time for that money.

When you have enough of these investments, they pay you're your basic financial needs. In other words, you're free. The diagram on the next page shows the progression business owners MUST achieve if they want their business to reach its full potential in the marketplace – plus make the impact it deserves. The Captivity Challenge, most business owners get imprisoned by trading their time in exchange for money. Your mission (should you choose to accept it) is to move into The Freedom Solution by building your Freedom Generator.

Entrepreneurs "buy back their time" by creating a Freedom Generator; a collection of cash flow positive investments.

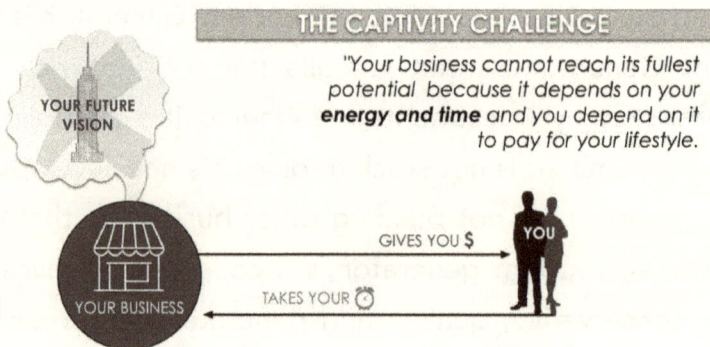

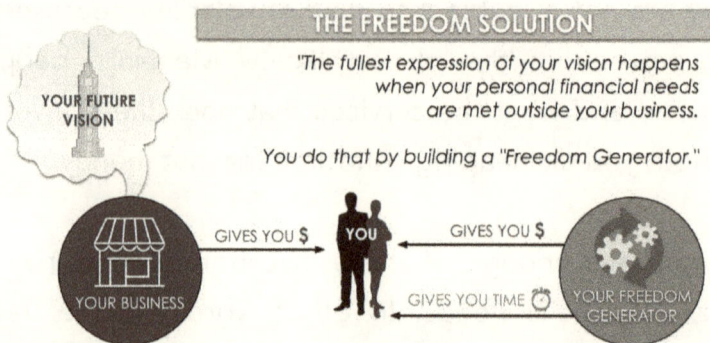

THE CAPTIVITY CHALLENGE

*"Your business cannot reach its fullest potential because it depends on your **energy and time** and you depend on it to pay for your lifestyle.*

YOUR FUTURE VISION

GIVES YOU $

YOU

YOUR BUSINESS

TAKES YOUR ⏰

THE FREEDOM SOLUTION

"The fullest expression of your vision happens when your personal financial needs are met outside your business.

You do that by building a "Freedom Generator."

YOUR FUTURE VISION

YOUR BUSINESS

GIVES YOU $

YOU

GIVES YOU $

GIVES YOU TIME ⏰

YOUR FREEDOM GENERATOR

You may run a personal services business, a manufacturing business, software business or anything in between. If your business requires you to show up and exchange your time to create value, your potential for creating freedom is at risk! Limited Freedom can exist within that plan. If you design your business carefully, you can get some time Freedoms but you aren't truly free yet.

You may have more flexibility and choice than the average person. That's true. But at the end of the day, if you need to exchange your time for money in your business, you're not 100% Free. For many business owners, what they have is the Freedom to spend more time than the average person does and earn less personal income because they pay themselves last and they serve everybody else first. You're taking enough risk in your business. The aim is to get money out of your business to build a personal Freedom Generator that contains quality, conservative, diversified, cash flow producing investments.

How to Create a Freedom Generator

Tony and I (Makaylah) are frequently asked to speak at seminars about Financial Freedom. I rarely accept these offers because the most valuable objective in my life is time with my family, and I'd rather be with my family than doing anything else.

However, when I accept an offer to speak; I usually begin by asking the group, "What if you could clone yourself, and could make that clone get a job and work for you? Every two weeks, when they get paid, they give you the check that pays for all your living expenses and you never had to work for money again... Raise your hand if you'd want one of those?"

Of course, virtually everyone raise his or her hands. Picture that for a moment. If you could clone yourself, and you could tell that clone what to do; what would you say? Wouldn't it be great to tell that clone: "Go to school, get a good education to get a job with high pay, and exchange your time for money and cover our expenses." That way, you wouldn't have to do any of that stuff yourself!

Instead, you could spend your time, worry-free, thinking of new ways to create the most impact possible. You could maximize your personal creativity. The great thing is: you can create that clone. That clone is your *money*. Your money is the thing that can go out in the marketplace and work hard for you. Your money is the thing you use to produce your own Freedom Generator.

Colin Campbell is a copywriter who assisted Tony and I to clarify the structure of this book you're reading now. He lives in British Columbia and his business model is a classic example of one that's based on time-for-dollars. Even though he loves copywriting, and he's skilled at it, his personal time is required to earn income. During one of the interviews with Colin he asked Tony, "OK... So, I understand in order to fully express your gifts and talents you need a Freedom Generator, which is a collection of cash-flow-positive investments that cover your monthly expenses... but, which specific group of investments should our readers make in order to do that?"

That is the most common question we get from business owners who are still working to build their Freedom: "Which specific investments should I make to create my Freedom Generator?"

The first answer is: that's not the best question to ask. People get road-blocked, attempting to "Discover the Secret Methods of Financial Freedom... In 90 Days or Less: Guaranteed!" They want to be told which safe, cash-flow-positive investments to make. The reason most people are not Financially Free is not because they lack the knowledge of which categories of investments they could make. The answer to that concerns is simple: invest in the things people buy regardless of the economy.

The better question is: "how do I change my mindset and habits to define and follow a financial plan long enough to become Free... then, maintain that plan long term?"

In addition, this book is not designed to be a "how to" guide on making investments. We're showing you how to structure your business in a way that accelerates your personal Freedom. What we can (and will) teach you is the fundamental process of investing — how to use your own mind to make the best decisions when it comes to your investment choices. As a result, you will become Free by using your own mind and creative process. As the saying goes, "give a person a fish: you feed them once. Teach a person to fish: you feed them for life." In other words, it's better to develop the mindset of investing over being told which investments to make.

The process of investing for Freedom is so simple it can be taught in less than 5 minutes. In fact, it's so basic: Tony's 20-year-old son does it with automatic, self-correcting efficiency (he does it on his own, and he succeeds without Tony). Still, to satisfy your desire about which specific investments to consider we've included a special gift for you. In the Additional Resources section of this book there is a Freedom Generator Checklist you can access online. It comes with a video training that shows the 5 principles of successful investing. Be patient though. It is important to read this book in the order we've placed it to get the highest (fastest) impact from it. If you skip ahead and go straight into tactics, we can almost guarantee you won't succeed as fast, if at all. Take your time to understand each part fully; success is a marathon, not a sprint.

CHAPTER #4

HOW TO TURN YOUR DREAM OF FREEDOM INTO REALITY

Now that you understand the three forms of Freedom and what a Freedom Generator is, take a moment and think of what your ideal Freedom future looks and feels like for you. It's important to understand that we've already begun laying a foundation of knowledge you'll use as we move forward into the 3 Phases of Financial Freedom in part 2 of the book. And, we still have some foundation to lay. How do you know you've built the future you once dreamt of if your "success criteria" is not clear from the beginning? The process of identifying and designing a clear Freedom Vision enables you to structure your business according to your real desires. It's like we're creating a filter that gives you <u>more of what you want and less of what you do not want</u> as you progress. The clearer you are on defining what your ideals are, the easier your success becomes.

The Impact of Freedom: What's Yours?

Allow your mind to think about the long-term vision for your business. Think about the impact you want to create in the

World as a result of your business existing in the time that you're alive. You may even think beyond your life. Do you want your vision to have a life beyond yours? A legacy?

As you think about the long-term vision, don't worry about how you'll create it yet. Forget about the steps involved to accomplish that future, just think about the main outcomes. Do your best to get a clear picture in your mind of this dream-come-true future. Think as BIG about your vision as you possibly can. In other words, don't think of the acorn, think of the forest. Allow your imagination to dream of the maximum limit that your business could become. Also, set aside your personal needs from the business for a moment focus on your vision for the contribution your business makes in society. It's difficult to address the two together, so the way to get the most authentic answer is to consider each of them separately, which is what we're going to do.

You might be building a business to last beyond your lifetime. What is its greatest impact? What service does it do to the community, to the world, to its clients? What impact does it make?

What do you want to exist in the world when you're dead and gone? What involvement and impact do you want to have as apart of creating that? As we write this, we're working with people who – one of their visions for business – is to eradicate sexual abuse around the world, which is a big and important vision. In our case, our vision is to create a new normal behavior in the world in the way people think about money. We want to completely cure money stress in the world and have a situation where financial literacy is something that is just normal, a world where people are creating their personal Financial Freedom from the day they make their first dollar.

Whether those results actually occur is not the point of this exercise. Don't place pressure on your imagination: empower it to flow. The point of this exercise is to expand your mind far beyond what your current reality is now, to allow yourself to dream further than you have in the past. As we mentioned at the beginning of this chapter, this process develops criteria for how you want to spend your time in the future. It also engages your spirit to make success mean more than just money.

Consider the following questions, one at a time:

- What is the fullest impact (or the fullest expression) that your business could make in the world?
- Does this vision expand and live beyond you or does the vision purely exist while you do?
- In what ways could your business specifically benefit more people's lives?
- Explain your grand vision for the business?

More/Less + Start/Stop
Creating a Breakthrough to Fulfillment

Okay, great, now that you're clear on your vision, let's take a look at what Freedom actually looks like for you personally. Every year, MindShift.money attracts groups of highly motivated and successful entrepreneurs who want to take their life and their business to the next level.

Of ALL the tools, strategies, tactics and methods we share at MindShift.money: the one we're about to share with you creates the most profound breakthroughs for the business owners who use it when thinking about their future, and how they want to live in this world. It's such a simple exercise too. This exercise is called, "The More/Less/Start/Stop Fulfillment Formula," and it's composed of four powerful questions you ask yourself (at any moment) when you want to gain clarity around what matters to you and what's most important to gain greater more fulfillment, from a true place not clouded by any financial stress or obligations.

First, we'll set up the environment in which we will answer these 4 key questions. Imagine this: you no longer had to work for money – imagine money came into your bank account every month and covered your monthly expenses. Your time could be used any way you please. Your role in your business could be whatever you choose. You could spend time in your business any way you choose. Imagine money wasn't an issue and you didn't need any money to come to you personally from your business -- because you have money coming in from sources that don't involve your time, effort or energy . With this in mind, you are now ready for the 4 most powerful questions you can ask and answer to boost fulfillment in your life. The entrepreneurs who answer these four questions (and act accordingly to what their answers are) become like beacons of light for the people around them. This is also a great process to walk your team through if you have one.

If you made enough money to cover your personal expenses, you didn't need your business to give you money:

1. What would you be doing MORE OF? What would you do more of in your business? What would you be doing more of in your personal world?

2. What would you be doing LESS OF? What would you be doing less of in your business and perhaps less of in your personal world?

3. What would you START DOING? What projects or causes or things that you're passionate about would you start doing?

4. Finally, what would you STOP DOING? What would you stop doing in your business and what would you stop doing in your personal world if money was not a concern?

You deserve this lifestyle of Freedom. You can live the reality you just envisioned. Having the Freedom to choose how you spend your time is likely one of the reasons you started your business in the first place. You took the leap to build a business and likely took a lot of risks in order to do it.

So why not create the true Freedom that allows you to take action to make the changes you just identified? Having your money handled, receiving money predictably from outside of your business is the next level to the Freedom you've worked hard to create so far. Freedom that truly gives you choice. Creating this next level of Freedom is truly is possible. You can proactively design and plan the life that you wish by creating your personal Financial Freedom. When you have enough income coming in outside your business, outside of your time, outside of your work... Then, and ONLY then is the full potential of your vision possible. In other words: *The full potential of your vision can only happen when your personal financial needs are met outside of your business.*

As you likely experienced from the exercise, you think differently when money is not a factor. You can see new possibilities when making money isn't the top priority. You have access to your full creativity and imagination when you are no longer worried about bringing money in. This allows you to see a much bigger vision rather than just a fraction of what's possible. Meeting your personal financial needs outside of your business allows you to create the full potential of your vision. How you do that is by building your own personal Freedom Generator.

A Story of Freedom

We spoke previously about the type of members that are a part of our Business Owners only global community within MindShift.money. These people are gifted luminaries, fulfillment oriented, and passionate about the impact their business can make in the world. They understand the value of becoming Free so they can help the world in a bigger way.For this book, we made a point to interview some of the people who are a part of this Business Owners only community in MindShift.money.

Everyone we interviewed has achieved complete Financial Freedom in his or her life, or are actively on their way to Freedom and have begun experiencing the edges of a Freedom lifestyle, so you can be sure the information they share in our interviews is coming from authentic experience, not theory.

Andrew Rezmer is our dear friend and peer who we highly respect and we'd like to introduce you to him as our first Freedom Story. He is a serial entrepreneur, philanthropist, angel investor, and thought leader. Enjoy Andrew's story...

Freedom Story: Andrew Rezmer

It's really difficult to define my occupation. I don't really have one. I'm owner of and creator of about 30 different corporate structures; all have different forms of businesses within them. Basically all my businesses are focused on fulfilling Maslow's Hierarchy of Needs for people in the world. I have businesses that are related to shelter and homes. I have businesses related to food and safety. Businesses related to inspiration and education.

I became financially Free for the first time in my twenties. I lived in Poland. Back then $15 per month was all I needed to cover my basic living expenses three times over. I know that sounds crazy now, but that's what it was. Even though it was a socialist country, I lived a capitalist-like lifestyle.

When I arrived to Canada I had to start from scratch. I had my few thousand dollars that I brought with me, but that meant nothing. That money practically disappeared from my hands. A couple months later I had nothing.

I had to start again from scratch. I started the same way I always do. I started creating some businesses. Within 2 - 3 years being in Canada, I was financially independent again.

I realized, since I don't have to work anymore, what should I do with my time? What should I my life? My expertise? My wisdom? My passion? Naturally for me, the outcome of those thoughts was how could I serve more people? How can I help? How can I give? My biggest transformation happened when I realized: To live is not to get more? No. To live is to give more.

Makaylah: When you created Financial Freedom, what did your Freedom Generator consist of?

Initially, I started with a few small corporations. The biggest financial transformation was with investments in companies and real estate. That's where I created the biggest impact in creating my financial Freedom. Also, I've learned most (about offering value to the marketplace) through real estate. That's why I invested my time and energy to become an expert in finding and structuring amazing real estate transactions. We structure the deals in a way that helps other people – people who ordinarily would not be able to afford a home of their own. We created a unique process to match those people with home sellers. Between marrying those two needs, I've put myself in the middle and created a very lucrative and conscience business.

Makaylah: Do you believe that creating and obtaining Financial Freedom is attainable?

Yes! I was born into a family with just my mother, who was working very hard. I had no other forms of ways to fulfill my dreams or buy anything, unless I made that money myself. I think I was probably 8 or 9 years old when I started my first businesses. I started small, selling stuff to kids in my neighborhood, you know. That stretched and progressed from doing small, kind of casual work or projects, to structuring ongoing projects when I was a teenager. I believe <u>anyone</u> who has a desire to help people, and use financial structures like the ones you guys teach will inevitably become Free.

Makaylah: What advice would you give to people who believe having their money work for them and becoming Financially Free is only something financial geniuses can do, or is a scam?

I'm not a financial genius. I'm not a scammer. I became Free by focusing on how to help people get what they want. After all those 50 businesses that are in the past and 30 that I still have; I still do what I'm passionate about. I recommend the same for others.

Do something that really makes you tick… Something that you gets out of the bed in the morning, not out of fear, but from a place of pure passion.

I can't wait to go out and make change in this world. I stay up late at night, not watching boring videos, but making contribution to this world in a way that actually makes me happy. That's the first step. Financial Freedom and financial outcome is just a natural result of following your dreams.

And, I would love to see a world where money isn't in the realm of anyone's worries. A world that is all about passion, happiness, kindness, compassion, giving, serving, providing. I feel that that is more important than anything else. I don't know if I'm answering the question, but I want to see a world based on love.

A world based on being kinder to one another.

We love Andrew!

What about you?

What new ideas, thoughts and insights did you get from Andrew's Story?

Before you move on and read the next chapter, take a moment and consider what Andrew shared and how you can apply his wisdom in your own business and life. Take a moment to pause and write down any new messages and ideas you've gained.

CHAPTER 5

THE "REAL" FREEDOM BUSINESS MODEL

In Chapter one we mentioned to you that as you read on, you'll see the overarching theme of this book is this: *Become conscious of every move you make in your business and direct your actions towards becoming personally Financially Free. Only then will you and your business be fulfilling your greatest and purest expression in this world, only then will the potential of the impact you can make in this world truly be realized.*

In other words, structure your business model consciously – by design and never by default – to result in your financial Freedom. This is your top, un-negotiable, most important PRIORITY. The reason you want to become Financially Free isn't just because being independent feels super amazing, and it enables you to spend your time however you want. That is just the sweet chocolate icing on the cake. There's something else more important that comes from you becoming Free: the cake itself. The more important byproduct of your Financial Freedom is that when you're Free (when you don't need to exchange your time for money) your ability to make a bigger impact in the world increases exponentially.

Andrew Rezmer touched on making a bigger impact in his interview and we want to re-emphasize the point. Your truest human potential can only be fully expressed when you break the connection between time and money. When you are coming from complete purity and money never enters (nor is considered to enter) the conversation. So, as a business owner: HOW do you do it?

You already know you have to build a Freedom Generator, but how you do that is by structuring your business model in a way that feeds your Freedom Generator. There are only two business models that exist with the power to do this. The models need to be structured in a certain way to reach that outcome, but when they are: financial success and personal Freedom is the only natural result. Introducing these two business models to the world is what we are calling The Business Model Revolution! We call it that not only because we like it and it sounds cool, but it is exactly what it is. It truly is a REVOLUTION.

Which Business Model Are You Building?

Let's take a look at the two REAL Freedom Business Models now.

The two types of Freedom Business Models are:

1. A Profit Business
2. A Legacy/Profit Business

Every business model that has ever existed or will exist fits into one of these two categories, as you'll see in a moment. There are no exceptions to this rule. The underlying structure may change from one business to another. For instance, one of the most basic examples of structural differences between companies is what they sell. An organic cat food company and an optometrist are probably the least similar companies in terms of their value offering to the market. One sells food to pet owners at a certain price point, the other helps people with their eye balls, likely for much higher fees.

One may sell its product online, while the other requires you to walk in to their office and have an examination. They both offer completely different benefits and have virtually no relation.
Still, the overarching business model of both companies could be a Profit Business OR a Legacy/Profit Business. We're going to break down the key differences of both models. The important thing to understand is that right now you are building one of these models. But, you may not be consciously aware of which one you are building. Most business owners are not.

In fact, most business owners believe they are building the Profit Business when they're actually building a Legacy/Profit Business. Plus: almost all business owners – 96%, as we mentioned at the beginning – are not structuring either business model to reach Freedom, regardless of which one they're building.

If structured properly, both business models will enable you to achieve Financial Freedom. Neither model is objectively better (or worse) than the other. However, your desires will determine which business model is more effective for you. That's why in the last chapter we explored what your true vision is for Freedom. If you know that, you know which model you should be building AND the way you should structure it.

Remember the fairytale Goldilocks and The Three Bears? The little girl, Goldilocks, thought one bowl of porridge was just right based on her personal preferences, and she gobbled up that porridge.

We are not directing you to create one business model over the other. We are indifferent to which model you create. We are helping you determine which model is just right for your desires, preferences and outcomes in your life.

Next, we're going to define what makes each business model what they are. What does one model have that the other does not? Then, you'll determine which one you're building.

Understanding which business model you're building is important because in Part 2 of this book, you'll learn how to customize your preferred model in order to achieve financial Freedom.

Which Business Model Are YOU Building?:

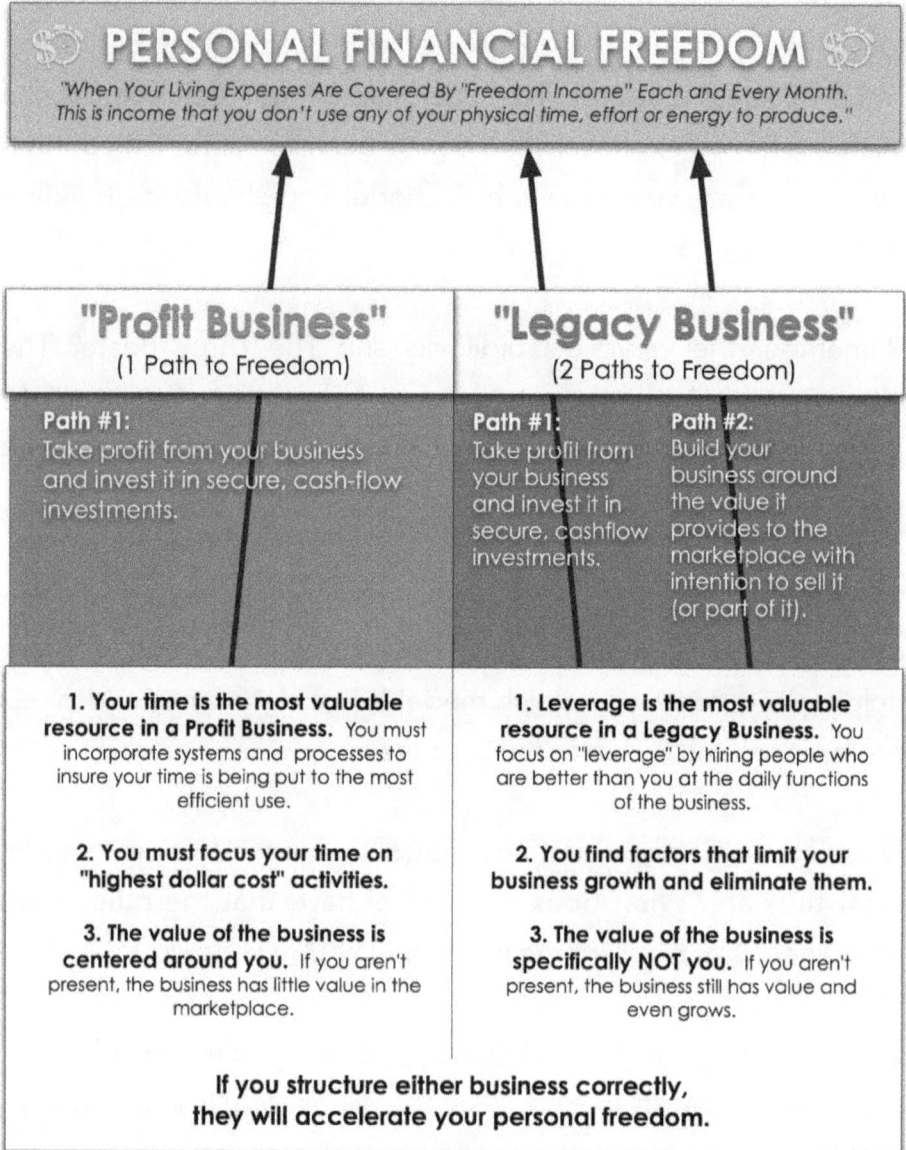

$ PERSONAL FINANCIAL FREEDOM $

"When Your Living Expenses Are Covered By "Freedom Income" Each and Every Month.
This is income that you don't use any of your physical time, effort or energy to produce."

"Profit Business"
(1 Path to Freedom)

"Legacy Business"
(2 Paths to Freedom)

Path #1:
Take profit from your business and invest it in secure, cash-flow investments.

Path #1:
Take profit from your business and invest it in secure, cashflow investments.

Path #2:
Build your business around the value it provides to the marketplace with intention to sell it (or part of it).

---

1. Your time is the most valuable resource in a Profit Business. You must incorporate systems and processes to insure your time is being put to the most efficient use.

2. You must focus your time on "highest dollar cost" activities.

3. The value of the business is centered around you. If you aren't present, the business has little value in the marketplace.

1. Leverage is the most valuable resource in a Legacy Business. You focus on "leverage" by hiring people who are better than you at the daily functions of the business.

2. You find factors that limit your business growth and eliminate them.

3. The value of the business is specifically NOT you. If you aren't present, the business still has value and even grows.

If you structure either business correctly, they will accelerate your personal freedom.

Defining A Profit Business

As you can see from the diagram on the last page, a Profit Business has ONE pathway to Freedom built within it, where a "Legacy/Profit Business" has TWO paths to Freedom.

In the Profit Business YOU are integral to the value of the business. This business model will not likely have a lot of intrinsic value – if any at all – due to it's inability to be passed to someone else and still make money. At some point you'll no longer be able to work and when that happens, this business will stop creating value in the marketplace. In fact, when that moment happens, there's over an 80% chance that your business will close its doors and not make money once you are not a part of it. The reason is because the value of the business lies with you being present. You are the center, a key player, or the key player in the business...when people come to the business they want to see you!

It is extremely hard for someone to replace you, and because of that, there'll be no real buyers if you desired to sell it for a lump sum of money. Even if you do find a buyer, it's unlikely they will give the amount of money that would be enough for you to build your Freedom Generator.

And there is nothing "wrong" with this model. In fact, a lot of people have become Free by creating a Profit Business. The pathway to Freedom for them, within this business model, is by continually increasing the profit. Your pathway to personal Freedom from a "profit" type of business is to structure regular withdrawal of profits along the way that you use to build your Freedom Generator, outside of your business.

The Most Valuable Asset
In A Profit Business

Well, the most valuable asset is your time. You are integral to the business. Time is the limiting factor in that business, so your aim is to have your time spent in the highest-dollar-cost activities possible. The aim in this business is to keep your expenses low, and your profits high, so the type of expenses you want to bring on board are expenses that allow you to maximize your time. You're looking for things that allow you to take your non-productive activities away from you.

Examples of support systems that provide you more efficient use of your time may include:

- Support staff
- Support processes
- Automatic appointment systems
- Automatic reminder or engagement emails
- Systemic ways of running your business

All those examples are ways that take non-productive activities away from you and place them on someone else (or technology) that you can pay to acquire. That way you can have a higher proportion of your working time allocated to the highest-dollar-cost activities. Everything else is unnecessary for you to be performing with your own time.

It's important for you to remember that right now our objective is to define the difference between the two types of business model and help you determine which one you're building so you have a clear path to Freedom. In Part 2 of this book we're going to dive into more specific ideas about how you structure either model to build your Freedom Generator, including product offerings and pricing models. Right now we're reviewing the thumbnail sketch of each model to lay a foundation for us to build upon together.

Defining a Legacy/Profit Business

As we go forward, we're going to refer to the second business model as simply a "Legacy Business," to reduce confusion between the two. There is one major factor that is unique with a Legacy Business (and accelerates your personal Freedom). That unique factor is that you are NOT integral to the value of the business. This is vitally important to differentiate the two types of business models from one another.

The aim, specifically, of a Legacy Business, is for you to become an insignificant part of the everyday functions of your business. Ultimately it is designed for the business to thrive and grow independent of your personal effort. In fact, the mantra we came up with for our roles in the movement at MindShift.money is this: "Every day we become less relevant to the success of this mission." We want to become less relevant because our desire isn't to build just another successful company.

Our mission is independent of us and lives beyond us, its to create a new normal around money in society. This type of undertaking will only become a reality as we place less attention on ourselves and more attention on systems that can multiply our message through technology and people. Right from the beginning, we knew a Legacy Business is the only option for us to achieve our objective. It is the guiding principle that determines everything we do. That's why we placed so much emphasis on vision, purpose and impact in the beginning chapters. When you're clear on your impact, this Business Model stuff reveals itself automatically. Wanting to influence and reach twenty million people is a very different model then wanting to influence and reach ten people who influence two million people each. See the difference?

We would identify that wanting to reach twenty million people is most likely a Legacy Business Vision and wanting to reach ten people (who reach and influence two million people each) is most likely a Profit Business Vision. In both cases the aim is to impact 20 million people though they accomplish this using two distinctly different models and structures of measurement.

How One Sale Can Make You Free

With a Legacy Business at some point you're planning on having the business run without your involvement. That's the key aim. Also, at some point, you'll probably want to sell the business, and that can happen a lot of ways. You could sell the business to your existing staff. You can sell to external buyers. You could list it on the stock exchange and sell it back to its members. There is a range of different ways to sell part or all of your business, and a range of different ways a business is valued to the buyer. Every case is different.

The pathway to Freedom in a Legacy Business is to sell part or all of it and build your Freedom Generator in one go, or largely in one go, from this type of business. Plus, just like a Profit Business, you structure this model to take out profits along the way. Hence, when we first teach the concept we're clear to call it a Legacy/PROFIT Business. If you're able to pull some steady profits along the way, you end up reducing the risk on the value that you need to get from the end sale of your business.

The most valuable asset in a Legacy Business is not your time. You're specifically trying to buy your time back in chunks and pieces of the business. The most valuable asset in a legacy business is leverage. It's systematically looking for the things that limit growth of the business, and unlocking those pieces.

The key aim here is to develop new systems and hire staff who are more skilled than you are. That means is you'd likely be spending more money in the early days to leverage, so in the early days, your profit is likely to be lower. This leads us to another distinction of both business models...

The "Profit Pathway" of Your Business

Basically, The Profit Pathway is the way in which each model earns money. The following diagram illustrates The Profit Pathway of each business model:

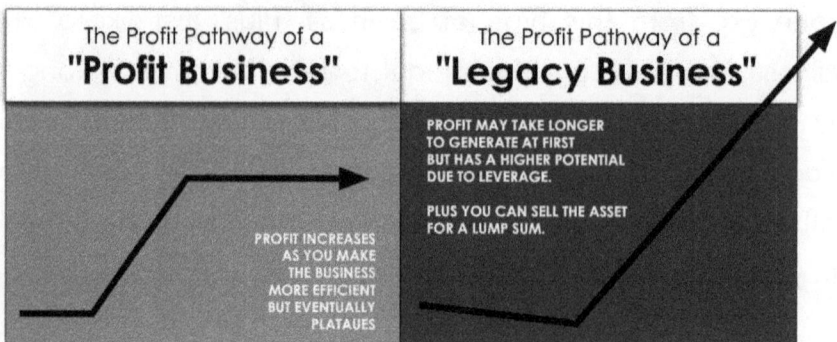

The Profit Pathway of a **"Profit Business"**	The Profit Pathway of a **"Legacy Business"**
PROFIT INCREASES AS YOU MAKE THE BUSINESS MORE EFFICIENT BUT EVENTUALLY PLATAUES	PROFIT MAY TAKE LONGER TO GENERATE AT FIRST BUT HAS A HIGHER POTENTIAL DUE TO LEVERAGE. PLUS YOU CAN SELL THE ASSET FOR A LUMP SUM.

The likely Profit Pathway of a Profit Business is as follows:

- Profit starts coming in, builds up, and then it plateaus out as your time is maximized, as there are no more ways you get more efficient with your time. Dependent on you, the pathway to Freedom is steady profit along the way. Again, the most valuable asset in a Profit Business is your time.

The likely Profit Pathway of a Legacy Business is as follows:

- You're likely reinvesting in a Legacy Business to build up your systems and processes. The profit will go down to start with before it starts going up. But then, if you've successfully removed your choke points, its profits can go far higher than what they could in a Profit Business.
- Once your systems are working and you can scale a Legacy Business, you can quantify how much money it's earning without your involvement, thus making it attractive for a buyer. When you want to sell the business you'll receive a large lump sum of money that you'll use to fund your Freedom Generator.

These two considerations may make you wonder... Which Business Model is "Just Right" For You? As we mentioned both business models would lead you to Freedom based on how they are structured to build your Freedom Generator.

For example, my (Tony's) brother started his career as a mortgage broker, which at the beginning was a Profit Business and everything functioned around his personal effort. He brought on a partner so they could share the cost of an assistant and combine their efforts. That's an example of how he maximized his dollar cost average. Once he had an assistant, he didn't have to schedule his own appointments and some of his emails were answered without him needing to use his personal time to do so. Still, his time was required to speak with clients and bring in revenue.

From the beginning, he structured his Profit Business to take a portion of the profits and build his Freedom Generator separate from the Brokerage. It wasn't long before he was earning a multi six-figure income due to the systems that steadily increased his efficiency. Eventually he maxed out his income because his time was so efficiently used, he couldn't possible squeeze more revenue without having himself cloned. At that point, my brother and his partner designed ways to take their existing model and transform part of it to be a Legacy Business.

They discovered a way to license their intellectual property to other people in their same industry. At first, they had approximately five people who invested in their system. There was no obvious sale value of any major nature at that point in time but my brother and his partner used the additional profits to contribute to their Freedom Generator. That decreased the amount of time it would take for them to become Financially Free. Eventually, they extended the licensing business full out. They created a platform and they had 1,400 licensed mortgage brokers running through their company in Australia. Then they sold to one of the larger financial services firms in Australia for over one hundred million dollars.

ZANG!
One sale: Financial Freedom.

As you can see, my brother's financial Freedom was structured into his Profit Business from the beginning. For some people, that's exactly what they'll do. They are never inclined to build a Legacy Business and they don't have to. Their Freedom is structured into their business from the beginning. They'll use the 3 Phases of Wealth (which you'll learn in Part 2) to structure their Profit Business to result in Freedom. However, in my brother's case, he wanted to design new ways of accelerating his date with Freedom. In fact, that wasn't his main purpose. The reality is, he LOVED the licensing model because it was more in alignment with his gifts and talents and impact. So, while still maintaining his Profit Business, he developed that Legacy Model that offered a tremendous opportunity to the people in his marketplace. Within the new model his personal effort became less irrelevant to the business' success. That enabled him to evaluate it and sell it, acquiring all the money he needed for his Freedom generator. He achieved Freedom in one sale. Yet Freedom was something that would have happened anyway whether he built the new business or not. It's all in the structure. We mentioned at the beginning of this chapter, one of the grave mistakes many business owners make is thinking they're building a Legacy/Profit Business, when in reality they're building a Profit Business. The error comes from the lack of intrinsic value in a Profit Business because it's based on your personal effort. If you're building a Profit Business in the hopes you can sell it at some point in the future for enough money to retire on, that is not a good strategy. Hope is not a plan for Freedom. If you don't make Freedom your priority, and fail to double-check what you're building is of value: at the end of the day, there's nothing of value to sell.

Freedom Exercise

Think about your business and ask yourself if you're building a Profit Business or a Legacy Business. Recall the fullest expression of your business, your vision that you created earlier and the impact you want your business to make in the world. Within that vision, do you see yourself as an integral part of the business, or are you seeing yourself as being increasingly irrelevant in the business?

What type of business are you building? Let's make a decision, and be specific about which side of the equation you're actually on right now. Knowing this now will make a big difference as we move forward. Take some time to do that now before reading on. Now you've identified the type of business that you're building, yahoo! So, how do you actually go about building its true value? How should you structure it, and make sure that you're putting your time, energy, and effort into something that's going to create your Freedom Generator?

There are three phases that must be completed to structure your business model in a way that makes you Financially Free. In the next chapter we're going to give you an overview of the three phases to lay a foundation as we walk through the specific steps in later chapters. Everything you've learned so far is beginning to compound. Each part is related to the next.

Once you go through the 3 Phases to Freedom you will be positioned to build your personal Freedom Generator, using your business as the accelerator it is meant to be. You will also eliminate your money stress from your life (both in your business and personal worlds). Most business owners don't know what steps are required, in what order, to build their Freedom Generator. They attempt to learn based on their own trial and error costing them time, money and energy.

Even if you know your destination is Freedom and you have chosen your business model, without following the 3 Phases in the next chapter, it would be like driving blind with no GPS to a destination.

I (Makaylah) tried that recently in Calgary, Canada, and it didn't turn out so great. We were going to a friend's house for dinner and it was 9pm because our plane landed later then we had expected. We had no phone signal as we had just come from Australia, so we couldn't access the GPS. We knew the destination we were going to, but we were driving without any directions or idea of when to turn and which way. We drove for over 2 hours trying to find our friend's home and eventually arrived for dinner at 11.30pm. When we got back to our hotel later that night and connected our laptops to the hotels Internet we discovered that the destination was exactly 4 minutes away from the point at which we started.

Without a GPS, we added a total of two hours and twenty-six minutes to our journey that could have only been four minutes.

That's like delaying your date with Freedom by twenty years because you tried to build your business model without using our GPS to Freedom – "The 3-Phases of Freedom."

CHAPTER #6

WHY CREATING FREEDOM IS LIKE A TROPICAL ISLAND VACATION
(Ahhhh... Nice!)

In this chapter you're going to get an overview of the three phases that will take everything you've learned so far and help you apply it in your business. These three phases are like a guide to transform your business into an accelerator to personal Financial Freedom.

Imagine for a moment that in a couple months you want to take a two-week vacation to a tropical island. You've been working hard lately and it's time for Pina-Colada on the beach. So you go online and type in, "Top 10 tropical islands to take a vacation," and your search results are met with countless links to choose from. You surf the web and find many travel blogs, tourist websites, and videos that tell stories of all the places you could choose. While you're inspired you call your best friend and ask them if they'd like to join you on the vacation. They accept! You and your friend narrow down your selection to three different places: Puerto Rico, Bora Bora, and Hawaii. Then you ask

89

yourselves more detailed questions about the type of specific experiences you'd like to have while you're away. Do you want to stay in a hotel, or would you like to stay in a private shack for a rustic feel? Do you want to hike up a mountain, or would you prefer to take day tours on buses? Are there any well-known attractions you'd like to visit while you're there? Are you into the party scene? Specifically, what do you want to spend your time doing?

After weighing out your preferences, you now have enough clarity to decide which location is best. You decide that you want to take your trip to Puerto Rico. Great! So, what next? First you secure your accommodations for two. Again, for this you select your accommodations based on certain criteria. There is a process you go through in order to find the perfect place to stay. Will the place be convenient to get to where you want to go? What are the different price points of each location? Will one be busier than another? Do they have WIFI? What are their ratings? Do they supply unlimited Pina-Colada's? You take into account many factors, but finally you book your accommodations and voila! You're confirmed! The next question you need to answer is how will you get there? Will you take a bus, train, plane, or a car? Plus: how will you travel around the local environment once you arrive? Do you want to rent a car? Maybe you'll take a donkey… or camel… or magic carpet.

There's no magic carpets left to ride, so it turns out the best option is taking a plane to get there. The next step is looking online or calling a travel advisor for plane tickets to Puerto Rico. Similar to every other selection process you've used to get this far: your plane ticket purchase comes from weighing out your options and making a final decision. When you arrive you want the Freedom to travel when and where you want without hassle, so you decide a rental car is the best choice for you... Although you did try your chances again in getting a magic carpet.

Finally! Everything is in order for you and your friend to enjoy a wonderful two-week vacation to warm and sunny Puerto Rico. Your Accommodations, plane ticket and rental car have been secured. You know when you're leaving, how you're getting there, what you're doing when you arrive and when you'll return home. You've planned best you can knowing that life will add its own unexpected and spontaneous flair along the way. Time to get your bags packed!

Your vacation day finally arrives. You get to the airport and are welcomed by a 3rd degree Q&A session from the border patrol people and actually begin questioning if you are in fact a criminal with drugs in your back pocket. You get on the plane, and before you know it: there you are, in beautiful Puerto Rico.

Then something unexpected happens. Ah, hello life!

When you get to the car rental building, they are closed. You look on your phone to find the number for a shuttle service. To your surprise, the only shuttles you can find cost a couple hundred dollars and you refuse to pay that much. You look down the road and see a sign that reads, "Scooter Rentals." You walk over to the small building and rent two scooters for you and your friends. They even include little trailers to place your bags on the back. You arrive at your accommodations and luckily they are open. You get your key to your room, unpack and rest. Over the next two weeks you meet new people. You go dancing. You eat delicious food. You see things that astounded you. You buy gifts for your friends and family back home. Your trip is everything you hoped it would be. Even the weather was close to perfect the entire time. Your experience was an overall ten out of ten. Good on ya'!

What Does This Have to Do With Your Freedom?

The steps a person walks through to plan and implement an island vacation are the exact same sequence they use to plan their Freedom into their business model from the very start. Think about it for a moment. If you review the story again, there are three distinct phases you go through. They are:

1. Picking a destination.
2. Choosing your method of transportation and strategy to arrive at your destination in a knowable timeframe.

3. Going on and enjoying the vacation experience, plus overcoming any challenges that occur along the way.

If you know where you want to go for vacation, and you know how you'll get there: then you will get there. Simple. Similarly, knowing where you want to go in your business, and planning how you'll get there enables you to predict when you'll arrive and what activities you'll do upon your arrival. The process to achieve a vacation and Freedom is the same... And since tropical vacations are so fun and enjoyable, why don't we make your journey to Freedom that way too!

Phase #1 to Freedom: Crystalize

Your Personal Financial Freedom is the destination. Transforming your business model to one that builds your Freedom Generator requires getting very clear on exactly what that destination looks like. Getting crystal clear is what happens in the first phase in our 3-Phases to Freedom called, "Crystallize." We call this first phase Crystallize that because it's crucial to Crystalize a set of specific outcomes in your mind. You must know where you are and where you're going if you're ever going to get there. You need to get clear on your current financial reality; how much money you earn, save, owe, spend and invest right now. Plus, you need to know exactly how much money is required for you to build a Freedom Generator that will create Freedom for you. Gaining crystal clarity around all of the things that relate to your Freedom is the key principle in the first Phase. Hitting a target you can't is next to impossible if you have no idea where the target is. If you want to arrive at a specific destination by a certain date, you need to know your numbers.

What is the end destination? Where am I now? What is my timeframe for getting there?

Luckily, determining your numbers does not have to be boring or an overly complicated process. We've made this phase super simple at MindShift.money, so every business owner can find out their numbers in a matter of minutes. Crystalizing your Freedom gives you a new sense of motivation and confidence in your business. You'll find having this clarity will empower you to create it as you have full awareness of what is required. No more playing small and being unaware of the truth of your financial situation. This phase lights a fire under you to make a real change, to create the Freedom you deserve.

Phase #2 to Freedom: Customize

Now you know where you're going. Plus, you know where you stand in relation to that destination. How do you know which vehicle will get you there in the timeframe you've clarified?

In other words, how do you "Customize" your business model to achieve your financial Freedom? The Customize Phase is like your GPS for financial success.

All phases are equally important. However, this phase is where we see most business owners act as conditioned robots, to put it bluntly. They follow the newest business trend or product frenzy and never consider how it actually fits into the design of their Freedom or the destination they defined in the Crystalize phase. As an example, we were at a high-level marketing mastermind and a woman asked the group to receive help in pricing her coaching service. Random numbers started flying through the air from virtually every person in the room…

The people who offered suggestions were all well meaning, and simply answering the question she had asked based on their own personal experiences. They were trying to help, but how could anyone know what her she should price her products and offerings without knowing her Freedom Number? Remember, "Your financial Freedom: this is your top, un-negotiable, most important PRIORITY." Everything – including your prices – must support that end. We've given an example here based on pricing, however, this is only one of many pieces that need to be designed and considered in the Customize Phase. We mention it now because probably 6 out of every 10 questions we receive in regard to business models is about the topic of how to price services and products. It's one of the biggest sticking points for many people, and one of the biggest traps business owners fall into. There is a system to create perfect prices and it's directly related to your Freedom Number, and the Business Model you have chosen. We can almost guarantee the pricing distinction you will learn is unlike anything you've seen or heard ever before.

When you learn this, 'secret,' you'll have absolute confidence your services and products are priced just right every single time, without fail.

The Customize Phase is the ultimate way for you to plan your Freedom, while also protecting yourself from the distractions of "everyone else's well-meaning advice," that has a way of distracting people from their course and trapping them inside the hamster wheel of business, forever.

#3 of Freedom = Monetize

You know where you're going. You've got you're map. Now you're going on the trip. How do you make sure you're on track to do all the activities you planned? The third, Monetize Phase, is all about implementing your plan from the Customize Phase and tracking your progress to make sure every step forward brings you closer to your Freedom and the destination you set in the Crystalize phase is met. As the name also suggests: this is where you make money. Your purpose is to:

- Increase the amount of money you earn each month.
- Increase the frequency (amount of times) you earn money each month.
- Reduce unnecessary expenses.
- Accelerate how much profit you can take from the business to build your Freedom Generator.
- And/or leverage yourself out of the business to the point of sale.

In addition to those objectives you also want to make sure your passion is always in alignment with the activities you spend your time on. That's another thing that you can measure. One of the big benefits to incorporating this phase into your business is that it enables you to consistently make more intelligent, informed, and strategic decisions in relation to:

- Time: when you should launch a new product or marketing campaign.
- Sequencing: which products/services you should focus on over others, and in which order they should be focused on.
- People: who you need to perform certain activities to make your business function in the most flawless way.
- Systems: technology/processes that increase the efficiency of time in your company and set up automation.

In the Monetize Phase you will witness your dreams come true. This is where the rubber meets the road.

Again, The 3-Phases of Freedom are:
1. Crystalize – know your destination.
2. Customize – create your plan to get there.
3. Monetize – make sure you get there.

This brings us to the end of Part 1. Congratulations for staying with us and committing to your Freedom. Now it's time to dig in and begin to move through these phases for yourself.

PART II
THE 3 PHASES
OF FREEDOM

CHAPTER #7

THE FIRST PHASE OF FREEDOM: CRYSTALIZE
(Part 1 Your Personal World)

The Crystalize Phase is about beginning with the end in mind and crystalizing what financial freedom looks like to you. By the end of this chapter you'll know the exact numbers unique to you that correlate precisely to your date with freedom. There are 4 key numbers, 2 personal and 2 business, and 2 timeframes that you need to know.

Here they are:
Your Personal Numbers
1. Your Baseline Lifestyle Number
2. Your Freedom Number

Freedom Timeframes
1. Your Maximum "Date with Freedom"
2. Your Ideal "Date with Freedom"
Your Business Numbers
1. Minimum Profit Number
2. Ideal Profit Number

These are the 4 key numbers and 2 timeframes that you need to know in order to be able to map a clear path to freedom. They'll also enable you see at any point in time where you are in relation to your freedom goal. In this chapter we're going to be covering your Personal Numbers and your Freedom Timeframes

A Deadly Misconception to Clear Up

The Goal Is Cash flow, Not Accumulation. There are a few important distinctions you must have in place before you move forward. Clarity around these distinctions will remove any confusion from the processes you will learn and will ensure we maintain the same understanding while we explore the 3 Phases of Freedom. The goal is personal financial freedom. This is achieved by building a Freedom Generator outside of your business, and not to take your whole working life to do it! That may sound simple but there are often misconceptions about the Freedom Generator.Your objective is to build your Freedom Generator that pays all your monthly expenses in your personal world (Destination: Puerto Rico).

In other words, cash flow from investments pays for your bills so you can do whatever you want with your time.

What's important to understand now is that <u>we do not mean:</u> accumulate a lump sum of money that will support you from "A" point in time to "B" point in time (AKA the end of your life). The general population is conditioned to think in terms of net savings or net worth, not cash flow. Their goal is to save enough money so when they're 65 years old (Point A) they will have enough accumulated wealth to cover all their expenses until they die (Point B). That type of thinking is dangerous, and more often than not, doesn't work! Besides, accumulating net savings to then eat through when you "retire" is just a death wish. Essentially, you are hoping and praying that by the time your net savings equals zero you are dead. 75% of people lose this game badly with all their investment nest egg gone within 5 years, leaving them to rely on family, friends, government or charity to pay for your monthly expenses. We need to have a much better plan than that!

What we <u>are</u> talking about is building a Freedom Generator that at its core contains a range of passive (i.e. requiring none of your time) cash flow producing investments AND building it beyond the point where it generates enough cash flow to cover your expenses forever. Not only does it then free up your time to do what you are most passionate about, but it can also look after you no matter how long you live AND you are able to hand your freedom generator, completely intact, to the next generation to further build upon…that's the secret to true freedom! Also, think about the word retirement? What is it exactly that you are hoping to retire from? Life? That's like saying at the point you retire you have nothing left to contribute to the world. Which seems odd to us.

So, we much prefer to have the Mind Shift of living fully with freedom until the day we die because all our expenses are covered and we can contribute to life fully in the way we personally design. In the model you are about to learn, you will discover how to use your business as an accelerator to building your personal Freedom Generator to the point where you <u>do not personally need any money from your business, because your Freedom Generator is able to produce enough cash flow to cover your personal needs.</u>

To clarify, it's more than okay for you to still have profits from your business, however you want to move beyond needing the profits. There is a big difference between choosing to run your business and having to run the business because you need the money. I hope that distinction is crystal clear now. That leads us to another important distinction. We touched on this topic earlier in the book, but it's important to cover it again in a little more detail. You are not your business.

There are two distinct parts to The Crystalize Phase:
1. Your personal world.
2. Your business world.

The first concept to grasp is that you are not your business and we need to separate your personal financial needs from your business' financial needs. For most business owners, one of their biggest mistakes is that they blend their personal and business financial worlds. That codependency between causes a weakness in both.

The most common example of financial entanglement between the two worlds is business owners who don't pay themselves a consistent salary. Anytime they need money in their Personal World, they go out and dip into their business money. In this world business owners very often find themselves personally underpaid chronically stressed and usually in personal financial pain.

Another common example of blending the two financial worlds together is dipping into personal savings to pay for business expenses. For instance, if an annual email database service fee is due, they go to their personal account and pay it. If you don't protect your personal money from your business expenses (or vice versa) it causes an inconsistent, unexpected burden on both.

How could you reliably secure your financial freedom in that scenario? You cannot. You cannot afford to maintain personal/business world contamination. The real price being paid is the price of your future freedom. Most business owners that are mixing their personal and business monies are so busy putting out personal and business cash flow fires that planning for their future freedom seldom exists in any meaningful way. You didn't get into business to live a life of stress. That's why you must put measures in place to separate and your personal finances separate from your business's finances. The question to answer here is: "How do we make sure you've got consistent personal income to cover your expenses today?" Then the next question is: "How will you structure your personal finances to achieve financial freedom in your future?" From this point forward we're going to address money in your Personal World separate from the money in your Business World. In fact, this Chapter is dedicated specifically to your Personal World.

Your Current Financial Pulse

Having a regular, predictable personal income is the key to laying a solid financial foundation that you can build to freedom from. As a business owner, this applies to you as well.

One of the first and most important outcomes from separating your personal and business finances is for you to be paid a regular predictable income from your business. Easier said than done though, right! So how exactly do you do this? Well it starts with crystallizing exactly what your personal income needs to be. As a result, in this next section we're going to map out your personal financial needs. By the end of this section you'll have Crystal Clarity around how much money you currently earn, save, invest and spend in your personal world. This is the first step to determine your Freedom Number, which influences all of the decisions you will make in your business going forward.

Step #1: Know Your Baseline Lifestyle Number

What we're going to do now is get an understanding of how much money you spend each month on basic living expenses. You're going to write down how much money you spend per month on each of the areas on the next page. Also, keep in mind:

- If an expense is not a monthly expense, work out how much it costs you each year, and then divide that number by 12 to get your monthly expense number.
- The key here isn't to plan how you're going to alter your finances to achieve your objectives. We'll look at ways to customize your plan to accelerate your results in the second Phase of Freedom.
- Make this is as accurate as possible, but don't worry too much if you don't know the exact number for each expense. A reasonable estimate will be good enough for this step.

Your Baseline Lifestyle Number

Fill out the following Baseline Expense Chart under "Amount of $ Per Month You Spend Now," Then you'll receive instructions to calculate your Freedom Number.

What You Spend	Amount $ Per Month You Spend Now
Debts	
Home Mortgage	
Investment Debts	
Credit Cards	
Personal Loans	
Other Debts	
Housing	
Rent	
Council Rates	
Body Corporate Fees	
Building/Content Insurance	
Maintenance	
Electricity	
Gas	
Water	
Pay TV	
Other	

What You Spend	Amount $ Per Month You Spend Now
Transportation	
Car Insurance	
Car Maintenance	
Car registration / Licensing	
Gas	
Parking/Tolls etc.	
Trains/Buses/Ferries	
Shopping	
Groceries/Food	
Personal Care	
Clothing / Shoes	
Newspaper / Magazines	
Gifts and others	
Pets	
Education	
School / Fees	
Other Education Expenses	
Childcare / Pre-school	
Health	

107

Gym / Sporting	
Membership	
Health & Personal	
Insurance	
Doctors/Dentist/Vet	
Medications / Eye care / Other	

What You Spend	Amount $ Per Month You Spend Now
Travel & Entertainment	
Holidays	
Meals out	
Movies / Music	
Alcohol / Cigarettes	
Activities	
Other	
Other Expenses	
Donations / Charity	
Advisor Fees	
Child Support Payments	
Other	
Other	
Other	
Other	

Now add all your current monthly expenses together and place that total amount below in "Total Current Expenses Now" category.

Total Current Expenses Now:	

Congratulations… If you took the time to crystalize all your current expenses, you now have everything you need to determine your Freedom Number on the next page.

Step #2: Calculate Your Freedom Number

"Freedom is a number!" Dr. Tony Pennells

When most people think of financial freedom, they tend to think of vague, non-specific feelings that they associate with what being free would feel like. For example, financial freedom is no stress; being able to spend what I like; being able to do what I want. The problem is that is not specific…and you cannot build a map to a non-specific destination (it's like saying "I want to take a trip somewhere, sometime….how do I get there?!).

Remember:
1. Financial freedom is about buying your time back.
2. You become financially free when your investments are earning enough money for you to live off and pay all your bills.

So what is your Freedom Number?

Your Freedom Number is the exact point at which you first have the option to buy back all of your time. It is the minimum amount of cash flow you need your Freedom Generator to be producing for you to have the choice to not have to exchange you time for money ever again. At this point you have succeeded in buying your time back…you are now free!

How much do you need in your Freedom Generator to reach your Freedom Number? To consider yourself financially free you would need to make enough passive income from invested assets to live off without ever having to sell the actual assets.

This is where you don't have to worry about your money running out. Your money gets sent out to work, it earns its wage (whether that's interest, rent, dividends, or profit), and then goes straight back out to work again. And the best part is that once you no longer need it, you can pass your money onto your kids, and it goes straight out to work for them. How much do you need invested (for cash flow) in your Freedom Generator to be financially free? The answer to this question also depends on two things:

1. How much money you need to live on each year (your Freedom Number); and…
2. What percentage investment return (or yield) you can have your money earning for you.

The simplest way to calculate how much money you need to be financially free is to divide how much money you need each year by the percentage of investment return. (If you're not sure what percent investment return you could realistically aim for without undue risk, I would suggest you plan for somewhere between 3-5%. This is quite conservative (I, Tony, personally aim for 5%) – in many investments you should be able to get more than this, but you need to make sure that your investments continue to grow in value at least at the rate of inflation after you have taken out your income).

Let's look at an example: Let say all your personal living expenses total $5,000 a month. So, your Freedom Number is $60,000 a year (your Freedom Generator needs to generate a minimum of $60,000 a year in passive income for you to be financially free). If you were earning a conservative 3% cash flow from your investments, how big would your Freedom Generator need to be in order to earn $60,000 each year?

The formula is simple:

60,000 divided by .03 = $2,000,000

In this scenario, if your Freedom Generator earned 3% cash flow annually on $2,000,000, you'd receive $60,000 each year to cover all our expenses. Can you actually achieve that? Absolutely. You own a business! But Financial Freedom is not a small goal. It requires focus, commitment, and a specific plan to follow. What I can tell you is that financial freedom is absolutely achievable if you are prepared to pay the price.

The great advantage you have is that you're a business owner! If you structure your business correctly, you can accelerate to freedom faster than if were just employed. And that's exactly what we'll show you how to do in the next part; the Customize Phase. But right now, let's calculate your Freedom Number right now. All you have to do is take your total monthly expenses you calculated at the end of Step #1 earlier in this chapter and multiply that number by 12 to get your annual expenses…

This gives you your annual Freedom Number (assuming that your current expenses are the minimum you need to cover to be financially free….but more on that later). Now let's work out how big your Freedom Generator needs to be to generating enough cash flow to reach for Freedom Number. You now take your new Freedom Number and divide it by .03 (this is the % cash flow your money is earning…you can change this if you like, but stay conservative) to get your Freedom Generator goal.

THE FREEDOM FORMULA			
Total Monthly Expenses Now:	_____	**X 12 =**	**FREEDOM NUMBER**
ANNUAL EXPENSES		**/ .03 =**	**FREEDOM GENERATOR**

See how simple that is? As I mentioned before, a 3% annual return rate on your money is a pretty conservative figure. Your number could be 1%, 2.3%, 14%, or 55%, whatever.

I strongly suggest that you set your expectations towards the lower end (as previously mentioned, I, Tony, use 5% personally), and the reason is because:

a. You don't want to place unnecessary risk on your hard earned money. There is a saying that "the return of your money is more important than the return on your money!" My, Tony, experience is that it is very possible for my Freedom Generator to earn above 5% in range of quality, long-term investments.

b. It's better to be conservative and hit your target than it is to be hasty and fail... I mean, this is your life we're talking about here; it's not a game of monopoly.

Key Considerations About Your Freedom Number:

1. The higher the percentage you earn from your Freedom Generator, the less of a lump sum you need, and the faster you'll become financially free....but, be careful not to be sending your money out to work in high-risk investments....it might not come back alive!!

2. Your monthly expenses will likely decrease as time goes on, accelerating how fast you can build your Freedom Generator. For instance, if you have children, when they move out: food costs, health care, education, and travel expenses would likely go down. The same thing happens when you pay off your debts.

3. Different financial vehicles can enable you to become free far sooner. This is only one example to get you

crystallizing your thinking on exactly how you can become free sooner.

4. Knowledge and mastery truly is king here! Surround yourself with others who are on the same journey and preferably further ahead. At MindShift.money we have a community of entrepreneurs who have already reached freedom through multiple different vehicles outside their business. Members have the opportunity to get real advice, case studies and experiences and feedback from people who are actually walking the talk. See the Additional Resources page for more details.

It's great to look at ways you can accelerate how fast you become free. However, I still maintain that achieving your Freedom Number should be based on conservative criteria.

Be bright and optimistic about your ability to achieve Freedom, but be conservative about how hard your money can work for you within your Freedom Generator. The strategies I'm sharing with you here are about creating a virtually impenetrable financial wall around you and your family so you can build long-term, intergenerational wealth that gets passed down long after you are gone. Plus, you'll enjoy that freedom while you're here too.

Next, what we're going to crystalize something very important that relates to your Freedom Number. We're going to connect your Freedom Number with time; becoming clear on when you want to have your Freedom Generator built by, we call it "Your Date with Freedom". This is also critical to have in mind for the next phase, the Customize Phase.

Step #3: Your Date with Freedom: Set Your "Freedom Timeframes"

Now that you know what your Freedom Number is, you're going to look at it through four different perspectives. In plain talk: you're going to set four difference goals - two Freedom Timeframe goals, and two Profit goals. Within those four goals your Freedom Number will not change as the end result. However, your timeframe to achieve that number will change, hence the phrase "Date with Freedom." Two of the four goals are related to your personal financial world. We'll set those goals in this Chapter. The other two goals are related to your business world, and we'll set those in the next Chapter.

Goal #1: Your "Maximum" Date with Freedom

The first perspective is in relation to securing freedom within an absolute maximum amount of time. Meaning at the bare minimum, you must have your freedom secured in that time. At some point in time we will no longer be able to work for money. Whether it's our mental health, physical health, a family circumstance, or something else that impacts our money...

Inevitably we will stop working. When that time comes, if you haven't got your freedom generator built, how do you live? How do you eat? If you don't have your Freedom sorted out by that time you're going to be dependent on family, friends, government, or charity. Statistically you start becoming medically unwell enough that you can't work, somewhere between 72 and 75 years of age. I'm not saying that will be you, I'm saying that based on statistics this is what happens to the average person and it's something to acknowledge. If you're pushing your number beyond that point, you're on potentially dangerous ground. For most people a healthy number to set as the maximum time-line to have achieved Financial Freedom by is somewhere between 55 to 65 years old. This maximum timeframe is also important to have in place because a lot of business owners go, "No, give me a big goal to shoot for... A BIG goal!" and I reply, "OK, you can have that AND lets at least be aware of what your maximum time is as well so you can be sure you end up winning in both cases."

Goal #2: Your "Speed of Lightning" Date with Freedom

When do you really, really want to be free? You may say two years, or five years, or eight years. You chose whichever timeframe you like as long as it excites you and gives you a sense of motivation.

116

You want to make sure this number is also in a sweet spot zone too. Saying, "I'm going build my Freedom Generator next year!" and being confronted with a massive wave of self-doubt and disbelief won't motivate you to get out there and win this goal. You want the number to be exciting, and at the same time within the parameters of your own sense of reason and Customized roadmap to get there. The first timeframe is a protection mechanism; to make sure that over time you're building an impenetrable financial wall around you and your family. The second goal, the shorter timeframe, is one that allows you to rewrite and redesign your life sooner, giving yourself permission to move and change directions and chapters whenever you want. So, what are your numbers? Take a moment and write both of your Freedom Timeframe numbers in the statements below. Say them out loud and look at them often.

"My Freedom Generator MUST be built
in a MAXIMUM of _____ years."

"My Freedom Generator
is IDEALLY built in _____ years."

Good for you, you just crystalized a clearly definable outcome in your personal world that – as a result of accomplishing it – will be game-changing in terms of the impact you can create in the world.

Summary

After busting some potentially devastating myths we now made a clear separation between your personal world and your business world. After that, we gained a specific snapshot of how much money you're spending each month on your personal baseline expenses. We took that number, turned it into an annual figure then calculated your Freedom Number. Then, we placed your Freedom Number in the context of two timeframes so we now know exactly when you are aiming to achieve personal financial freedom. One date was the maximum amount of time you want to achieve freedom within. The second was the "Fast as Lightning target, which is the ideal timeframe you have set to reach Freedom. In the next Chapter we're going to crystalize how your business is currently structured in relation to your freedom. We'll also set the two corresponding "Date with Freedom" goals within your business world and show you exactly how you business can act as the accelerator to produce your personal financial freedom. If you did the work we outlined in this chapter, congratulations! Having financial freedom as a clear destination, with clearly stated timeframes to get there is a pivotal and essential precursor to have in place first. All key decisions within your business need to align with this intention. As the saying goes: "If you fail to plan, you plan to fail." The amount of energy you put into this process is the exact amount you'll get back.

CHAPTER #8

THE FIRST PHASE OF FREEDOM: CRYSTALIZE
(Part 1 Your Business World)

In the last chapter we cover your 2 Personal Numbers and 2 Freedom Timeframes. In this chapter, we are going to be working out your 2 Business Numbers. As a little memory jogger, here are the 4 key numbers and 2 key timeframes again:

Your Personal Numbers
1. Your Baseline Lifestyle Number
2. Your Freedom Number

Freedom Timeframes
1. Your Maximum "Date with Freedom"
2. Your Ideal "Date with Freedom"

Your Business Numbers
1. Minimum Profit Number
2. Ideal Profit Number

By the end of this Chapter you will know exactly how much

profit you need from your business in order to secure your freedom firstly within your Maximum Freedom Timeframe, and then within your Ideal Freedom Timeframe. The first step is…

Step #1: What Business are You Building

In Chapter 5 we made a distinction between the two types of business model. Recall they are:

1. A Profit Business
2. A Legacy Business

You're either building a Profit Business (one with steady profits to contribute to your Freedom Generator, yet no probable sale value at the end of your working life), or you are building a Legacy Business (one with steady profits designed to be sold for a significant sum that will contribute entirely or partly to your Freedom Generator). The first step to ensure your business is structured properly to result in your financial freedom is not only knowing which one you're building, but also ensure either is structured in the correct way. Your business must be able to accomplish 3 things:

1. Provide value to the marketplace;
2. Provide you enough Personal Income for your current lifestyle; AND, over and above that…
3. Generate enough to build your Freedom Generator <u>outside</u> of your business!

We want you to pause and really consider the 3 points above. Can your business afford neglect any of these 3 things?

If they are not ALL built into your business plan, ultimately there will be potentially catastrophic consequences. Your Personal Financial Freedom MUST be Built into your Business Plan.

There is a saying that you must "begin with the end in mind". Never is that statement more true than in a business...and yet, the vast majority of business owners we come across have no clear plan as to how they will secure their personal financial freedom outside of their business. It is not surprising that most business owners are in chronic money stress, and very seldom are able to achieve personal financial freedom. Your Freedom Lives Outside of Your Business. Personal Financial Freedom outside of your business is ultimately the destination that your business must deliver. If you do not have this as a non-negotiable intention within your business, what are the chances that you will accidently stumble into financial freedom? Slim to none, right?!

The people who achieve financial freedom from their business actually have that strategically planned into their business models. It is no accident, and it is not luck....they begin with the end in mind.

So if you are going to begin with the end in mind of personal financial freedom, how do you plan that into your business model? Well, it starts with firstly being clear on which business type you are building...a Profit Business or a Legacy Business.

Then, you first need to know what profit target to achieve to be able to secure your personal financial freedom outside of your business within you Maximum Freedom Timeline. This is the Minimum Profit Number that you business <u>must</u> achieve for you to have any real chance of securing your freedom within your working life. But you want more than that right? You didn't get into business just to survive; you got into business to be able to thrive...to 'suck from the marrow of life'!

Your real abundant living will come when you no longer need any personal income from your business. THIS is what you want to aim for,...and you don't want to take your whole working life to do it. We all have much more important callings and contributions to make in our life far beyond working for a living. Lets aim to get this out of the way as fast as possible. And if you plan it correctly, you truly can use your business to accelerate to freedom far faster than everyday mortals...I mean people with a job ;) . So, secondly you need to know your Ideal Profit Number to secure your personal financial freedom within your Ideal Freedom Timeline. Let's find out what they are. You ready?

Step #2: Your Profit Numbers

Remember the two Freedom Timeframes you calculated for your personal world? One was the maximum amount of time you needed to achieve your freedom by, and the other was your "knock it out of the ballpark" goal (Ideal timeframe).
Remember what your timeframes are?

"My Freedom Generator MUST
be built in a MAXIMUM of _____ years."

"My Freedom Generator
is IDEALLY built in _____ years."

The two timeframes you already calculated are your personal targets to build your Freedom Generator separate from your business. The two numbers we're going to crystalize next will show how much profit your business needs to generate each year for you to achieve both of those personal timeframes. The example below assumes that you need $2,000,000 in your Freedom Generator to generate your Freedom Number; and your Baseline Lifestyle Number are $60,000 (which is the same number we used in the illustration in Chapter 7).

Important Note – we are keeping these calculations simple to facilitate learning of the principles and concepts. To more accurately determine your exact profit numbers to will need to include:

- An allowance for tax - we assume the profit numbers are after tax has been paid;
- A profit pay-out ratio - this is the amount of profit that actually gets paid out to you personally. (I don't believe that it is healthy for a company should pay out more than 75% of it's profits) and;
- Freedom Generator investment return – this is how hard your money in your Freedom Generator is actually working for you.

We cover these in more depth with tools to assist you within the MindShift.money business owner community (which we encourage you to join). We also strongly suggest that you have your business coach/adviser assist you to ensure that these are accurate for you. However, the moment you start even getting a ball-park sense of what your Profit Numbers are, you will be moving in the right direction....so, let's do it!

To keep the numbers simple, we're using 20 years as our Maximum Freedom Timeframe and 10 years as our Ideal Freedom Timeframe to build our Freedom Generator.

EXAMPLE: YOUR "MAXIMUM TIMEFRAME" PROFIT NUMBER	
YOUR FREEDOM GENERATOR:	$2,000,000
Divide your freedom number by your maximum timeframe:	/
YOUR MAXIMUM FREEDOM TIMEFRAME:	20 Years
Add your personal expenses:	+
YOUR BASELINE LIFESTYLE NUMBER:	$60,000
ANNUAL PROFIT (after-tax) TO COVER YOUR BASELINE LIFESTYLE & BECOME FINANCIALLY FREE=	**$160,000**
EXAMPLE: YOUR "IDEAL TIMEFRAME" PROFIT NUMBER	
YOUR FREEDOM GENERATOR:	2,000,000
Divide your freedom number by your maximum timeframe:	/
YOUR IDEAL FREEDOM TIMEFRAME:	10
Add your personal expenses:	+
YOUR BASELINE LIFESTYLE NUMBER:	$60,000
ANNUAL PROFIT (after-tax) TO COVER YOUR BASELINE LIFESTYLE & BECOME FINANCIALLY FREE=	**$260,000**

Notice how the amount of annual profit you need to in order to build your Freedom Generator increases as you make your Freedom Timeframe shorter.

PART 4: YOUR "MAXIMUM TIMEFRAME" PROFIT NUMBER	
YOUR FREEDOM GENERATOR:	
Divide your freedom number by your maximum timeframe:	/
YOUR MAXIMUM FREEDOM TIMEFRAME:	
Add your personal expenses:	+
YOUR BASELINE LIFESTYLE NUMBER:	
ANNUAL PROFIT (after-tax) TO COVER YOUR BASELINE LIFESTYLE & BECOME FINANCIALLY FREE=	
PART 5: YOUR "IDEAL TIMEFRAME" PROFIT NUMBER	
YOUR FREEDOM GENERATOR:	
Divide your freedom number by your minimum timeframe:	/
YOUR IDEAL FREEDOM TIMEFRAME:	
Add your personal expenses:	+
YOUR BASELINE LIFESTYLE NUMBER:	
ANNUAL PROFIT (after-tax) TO COVER YOUR BASELINE LIFESTYLE & BECOME FINANCIALLY FREE=	

This marks a critical junction for you in your career and in your life. Not only do you know how much money you need to become Financially Free, you also know the exact numbers your business has to produce (in profit) in order to secure that freedom within your Maximum Freedom Timeframe and your Ideal Freedom Timeframe. The final step in this process is determining what your quarterly and monthly profit targets are. Knowing those figures will enable you to compare your actual profits with the desired profit targets, revealing whether you are on track to your freedom goals and timeframes.

Before you do that, I want to remind you that you are AWESOME!

Some people, when they begin looking at these numbers, notice how far they are from their goal and they feel guilty, scared or worried about whether they'll be able to achieve it. If you feel that way, just remind yourself the purpose of this is to think accurately....to get crystal clear on your freedom plan. It's not about where you start...it's about where you finish that counts! Getting clear on where you need your business profits to be a vital piece and congratulations for taking the step!

In the next phase, the Customize Phase, you will be exploring how to structure your business, products and services, and pricing to align to these profit numbers. In *Think and Grow Rich,* one of the all-time blockbuster books on the topic of success, Napoleon Hill talks about Accurate Thinking. This principle is something the most successful and wealthy people on Earth use to their advantage, while everyone else follows The Latest Hype without thought.

In addition, one of the books that have inspired us at MindShift.money is Steven Covey's 7 Habits of Highly Effective People. In that book Covey gives a great analogy for doing what is important instead of what is urgent. He says to think about your important priorities as big rocks and urgent priorities as little rocks. If your life is a jar and you fill that jar with little rocks, you can't fit the big ones in. Financial freedom is important: it's a big rock. Allow thinking accurately to be one of your big rocks. It is important to know your numbers. That's what successful people do, and that's why you're doing it.

Knowing the score of any game is the first, most critical point of data you need to know in order to succeed. By knowing the score, you're taking a huge leap toward creating the impact you were designed to make using your life's energy. If you do feel discouraged at times, let it be present, but only for a moment… and then re-focus on your freedom destination take another step forward toward it. If you needed to hear that, we're glad you got it now!

Step #3: Quarterly and Monthly Profit Targets

The final move is to break down your new annual Profit Targets into quarterly and monthly "slices." To do this, you simply divide each profit number by 4 and 12. Following our example from before, our Minimum Profit Number was $160,000. We take that number and divide it by 4 to get our $40,000 quarterly profit goal. If we divide it by 12, we get $13,333 for our monthly profit goal. Do the same calculations below for your numbers...

PART 6: YOUR QUARTERLY / MONTHLY TARGETS			
MINIMUM PROFIT NUMBER		**IDEAL PROFIT NUMBER**	
Divide by 4 **Quarterly:**		Divide by 4 **Quarterly:**	
Divide by 12 **Monthly:**		Divide by 12 **Monthly:**	

Great! Now compare your minimum and ideal monthly profit goals with your current profit numbers and BINGO! You know exactly how much you need to increase in order to build your Freedom Generator within your Freedom Timeframes! Congratulations! If you're building a Profit Business, the process you just completed concludes the Customize Phase for you. If you're building a Legacy Business, we're going to take a couple moments to clarify some key considerations before we move into the second phase: Customize!

If you're building a Legacy business

With a Legacy Business, as we covered earlier, there are 2 potential pathways to freedom. The first pathway is profits over and above what you need for your Baseline Living Expenses that you are able to withdraw from your business and invest into your Freedom Generator over time. This is exactly the same as with a Profit business. The second pathway is through building a business that can continue without you (legacy), and is of enough value to someone else/another business, for you to sell some or all of the business for enough money to build your Freedom Generator from the sale. If you believe you are building a Legacy business, here are 2 very important points:

1. Make sure you have enough personal income to cover your Baseline Living Expenses; and
2. Be sure that what you are building truly does have enough potential value for you to be able to build your Freedom Generator from the sale.

So let's look at each of these in turn. You want to make sure first of all, you've got a consistent personal income to cover your Baseline Living Expenses. Then you'll most likely reinvest in your business for a period of time to build up its value. You may also forgo building your Freedom Generator from profits at the beginning because at some point in the future your plan is to sell a piece of OR all of your business to secure your freedom in part or in one shot. However, you want to be careful. Just because you feel like there's a bigger payday down the track doesn't mean it's true.

"Optimistic Entrepreneurial Delusionism (OED)," is a term we use at MindShift.money. It is a toxic disease that, when contrived, breeds other ailments like Shiny Object Syndrome and GURUitis. In business, OED can be more fatal than cancer. The entrepreneur who has this disease says, "Well I'm building a Legacy Business and I'm going to forgo building my Freedom Generator now. I'll reinvest in my business because when I sell the business: I'm free!" Sounds plausible...but in cases of OED, the entrepreneur hasn't done any serious checking to see if what they are building truly is of real potential value to some else.

Remember, it's not just about being able to sell the business...it's about being able to sell it for <u>enough.</u> This usually means a few million dollars, which is more than the average person walking around can usually come up with. Even if they are able to ultimately sell their business, if they don't sell it for enough, or the business fails to sell (which happens around 80% of the time), they haven't built their Freedom Generator. Then what do they do?

To avoid OED you get clear on your numbers, understand where the potential value truly lies in your business, and what your real opportunities are. That way you can make intelligent, informed decisions that have a real path to freedom, instead of random acts of hope. On the next page we're going to walk you through a questionnaire that will help you clarify where the value lies in your business, as well as establish when and why a buyer would purchase your asset, plus who that buyer might be.

As a result of this crystallization you'll be clear whether the option to structure your business for sale is actually a worthy consideration or just a whim. If you're already building a business to sell, the following questionnaire will give you keys to optimize how much you sell it for and help you avoid common pitfalls and blind spots that delay the sale process. Enjoy!

Legacy Business Questionnaire

Remember, there are pathways to building your Freedom Generator from both Profit and Legacy businesses. It is essential for you to be crystal clear which business you are building. The real risk lies in if you falsely believe that you are building a legacy business, only to discover at the end of your business life that it is of no value, or not of enough value to anyone else! If you can't give a detailed, well-designed answer to each of these questions: it's likely you are not building a Legacy Business model.

If at the end of this questionnaire it turns out that you are not building a Legacy Business, but that's what you want to build, then review the list of questions again. You can use it as a checklist to successfully create a Legacy Business that you can sell at some point.

Keep in mind that based on what you offer in the marketplace there may be more variables that determine how you sell it than the scope of this questionnaire could possibly cover. However, these are the "big rocks" you need to take into account before moving forward. If you have questions or desire specialized advice in regard to your specific business, please see the Additional Resources at the back of this book for information about MindShift.money. We offer additional education, training and community to help you master this in your business. We also have a platform of specialized coaches and advisers dedicated to helping business owners who want to grow, package and sell their Legacy Business.

Okay! Let's get right into the first question...

Question #1: "Who would buy your business?"
Question one, "who?" Be specific, put names down. You can either choose the general type of industries who may be interested in taking over your company or list specific company names. Preferably within your mix of companies, you'll want to

choose publicly listed ones, reason being that you can actually research what they're buying and why. So, the first question is, "Who would buy your business?" The second question is…

Question #2: "Why would someone buy your business?"
- Would they buy it for your people?
- Would they buy it for new geographic footprint?
- Would they buy it because they want some of your technology?
- Would they buy it because they want your franchises or your licensing?
- Would they buy it because they want access to your audience?

So, "Why would they buy it?" These are important questions to start thinking about, to work out where the value does or could rest in your business.

The third question is…

Question #3: "What would they value within the business?"
This differs to question 2. Question 2 is about why they would buy your business. This question is more specific about what they would place a tangible financial value on within your business.

This could include the following:

- Your Profit;
- Your recurring revenue;
- Your assets (e.g. property);
- Your database;
- Your trademarks and patents;
- Your franchise or licence contracts;
- Size of your audience (or unique monthly visitors to your website);
- And the list goes on.

Doing the research to understand this well before you are planning on selling, could ultimately add millions to your eventual value, simply because you are building something that you know someone wants to buy.

Question #4: "How do they calculate the value of the business?"

The fourth question is, "How do they value it?" For example, do they value it on a multiple of profit? That's the common one. They might value it on a multiple of recurring revenue. That's common in the financial services industry. They might value based on the number of unique visitors per month to your website. That's common in the publication industry (including online blog sites). They might value it based on how your platform could deploy through their client base. They might value it based on your number of clients and the possibility of cross-selling their products to that list of consumers. They might value it based on who your clients are and the possibility of developing strategic relationships with them to reach a broader group of new customers. Would they value it at five times your annual recurring revenue? Would they value it at three times, or would they value it at ten times? Having an idea on that number... That's why looking at a publicly listed company, that has acquired other businesses is very healthy is useful, because you can see on public record what a company bought, what they valued, how they valued, why they bought it, etc. You see that on a company's annual reports. So, there's a number of ways they can place value on your Legacy Business.

Question #5: "How much do you need from the sale to build your Freedom Generator?" Then, once you know those numbers you need to know how much you need to build your Freedom Generator. For example, if you know that you need $5 million to be able to build it, and you know that somebody would buy your business for 5 times of your recurring revenue, then if you get your recurring revenue up to $1 million, you know you're on track. You then just position yourself for sale. which leads us to the next question... But before you get too ahead of yourself – if you can't answer these 5 questions at least with a degree of certainty and facts, you are probably not building a Legacy Business.

It is safest to assume you're building a Profit Business until you can get clear on those answers and strategically build to something with a defined set of figures and values.

A Cautionary Tale

Again, I want to reaffirm something important. When we speak in detail about the benefits of building and selling a Legacy Business people often ask us: "Do you encourage people to move to a Legacy Business? Know where you are right now but look to build a Legacy Business as opposed to a Profit Business. Are you encouraging me to do that?"

No, we don't, that is an absolutely false assumption. Our personal natural bias leans towards building Legacy Business', because that's what we're building with MindShift.money. Our team is constantly creating new ways to systemize all our processes so ultimately MindShift.money can function and grow without us. That is the only way for us to make the largest impact as we can possibly make. The ultimate impact of creating global transformation of a new, financially healthy, normal is why we started the business. We began with that end in mind; and that guides every single action that follows. That's why we place so much attention on vision and purpose. We're encouraging you to use either Business Model to achieve your personal financial freedom outside of your business. That is the only absolute suggestion we make. We also give you the formulas, tools and strategies to accomplish your freedom through both Business Models because they are both viable options. For instance, a web designer who has no desire to build a business they can sell – who wants to earn money and do the work themselves – can achieve freedom potentially in less time by customizing their existing price structure, services they offer, or clients, or all three.

If that web designer crystalizes their Freedom Number, knows when they want to achieve freedom, and knows their numbers: they can achieve freedom. Period. We encourage people to seek their truth and reality. We encourage them to know where they're going and be honest and authentic about where they are in relation to that. Know what your pathway to freedom is. You can reach freedom through a Profit Business, and you can do it through a Legacy Business. What you can't do is think you're building a Legacy Business, reinvest, reinvest, reinvest in your business with no plan as to how you will get enough money out of the business to build your Freedom Generator.

You cannot just hope magically your freedom will come at some point in time because some angel will descend from heaven, look at you and say... "Oh my goodness, you've given so much of your life and your vision, and worked so hard, let me just take all your pain away and *BLING* [sound of fairy dust] here's your freedom!" That's Entrepreneurial Optimistic Delusionism. Just because your next-door neighbor, or that guy you met at a seminar, is building a Legacy Business shouldn't guide your decision as to which business model is right for you. You need to find your truth...your pathway to freedom outside of your business! In addition, note that your business doesn't have to be solely a Profit Business or a Legacy Business. It could have both within it.

A Profit Business can coexist within a Legacy Business, and a Legacy Business can coexist within a Profit Business.

The value that is part of your Legacy Business, could vest in multiple places in the business; and equally you might find that you're passionate about work that is your personal work, your personal brand going out there. This personal work is probably typical Profit Business territory, and will not live on without you....but...You could be passionate and not want to give that up. Doing this work could fulfill you in a deep and meaningful way that goes far beyond money. You don't have to give this up personal work if it is important to you. Equally, you can be simultaneously developing other areas in your business that are of high Legacy value. It just needs to be designed into your freedom plan. You could be doing terrific work yourself, plus have a licensing component that builds a platform that is of tremendous value, with an audience that controls the communication within the coaching marketplace, or spiritual-leader marketplace, or small-business owners of fish markets, or whatever. You can control that communication to that marketplace and have a publication voice with an audience. Have a licensed coaching site, which gives you that licensed platform of recurring revenue, plus have a component where your need for significance and value from what you personally do is completely taken care of as well…

… Oops! We got a little too excited for a moment there, because those different service levels are part of the Customize Phase, which is coming up in our next Chapter!

In this Chapter we crystalized how your business is currently structured in relation to your freedom. We also set the two corresponding "Freedom Timeframes" within your business and gave you a thought-provoking questionnaire on how to strategically sell your company if you're building a Legacy Business.

Congratulations for gaining an accurate evaluation of where you're going and where you are now…

YOU ARE OFFICIALLY
CRYSTALIZED!

CHAPTER #9

THE SECOND PHASE OF FREEDOM: CUSTOMIZE

By the end of this Chapter you're going to customize your business model to align it with the objectives you set in the previous Chapters. Here is where we create the plan to use your business to get you to Freedom. You'll likely notice how interconnected each Chapter has been to the next. So too is everything going forward. It works similar to building a house. If you don't build a concrete foundation first: you don't have anything to place the wood, plumbing, electrical, paint, or drywall onto. Because of that interconnectedness, this Customize Phase often creates the biggest revelations for business owners. After they clarify their Freedom Number and set their Date with Freedom in the Crystalize Phase, the very next question is "Ok, so HOW do I hit those numbers?" And the answer comes from customizing their business in a certain way. Once they clarify which customizations need to take place: a sense of absolute certainty, clarity and focus is the result. They know exactly where they're going and how they're going to get there. The reason this Phase is so profound to most people is because often it shakes them out of the thick smog of marketing we're exposed to as entrepreneurs, constantly telling us to focus on customizing our business FIRST. For instance, have you ever heard any of the following phrases?

- "Buy this email marketing course."
- "Get this landing page software."
- "Buy Facebook, LinkedIn, etc. ads."
- "Offer a subscription/membership service."
- "Learn how to speak stage and sell."
- "You should raise your prices!"
- "Get on news to build credibility."
- "Start a podcast."
- "Do a launch!"
- "Get you website SEO'd"
- "Start a coaching business."
- "Create a Survey Funnel!"
- "Write a book, a report, a mind-map, etc."
- "Learn how to write advertising copy."
- "Learn how to do a joint venture."
- "Hire someone overseas!"

All of those phrases are ways you can customize your business. Each could be great advice, but only under the condition that directly supports your Freedom. If they don't support your journey to your Freedom as you identified in the Crystallize phase directly, the action is likely not for you. So how do you determine which action is in your best interest? You must Customize your journey to Freedom.

We'll do that in this chapter. No more blindly following the latest hyped up marketing campaigns with no criteria to make strategic decisions. By the end of the Customize Phase you will be clear on what your path to Freedom looks like, through your business.

Establishing Your Criteria to Win

In order to focus on the parts of your business that have the highest impact on your Freedom, the first thing we're going to do is Clarify your "Magical Mix of Products and Services." We call it the Magical Mix because, in a way, it gives you special powers to predict and design your Freedom through the products and services you sell. This makes your Freedom a reality, almost as if by magic – a strategic magic show. Four criteria need to be considered in order to create your Magical Mix of Products and Services. When you have the right mix you will reach Freedom faster, your business will fulfill its greatest potential for impact and you will have the greatest fulfillment. Sweet, right?

To create your Magical Mix of Products & Services you will take each offering you have through four specific criteria. In evaluating each product or service against each criteria, you will have the right basis to create your Magical Mix of Products & Services that will serve you today and in your journey towards Freedom. I will give you an overview of the criteria now and in a moment I'll guide you through specific questions you can ask yourself to ensure you've got the best Magical Mix of Products for your business. Here we go...

1. Impact:

First you must evaluate how important each product or service is in fulfilling the fullest impact potential your business can ultimately have in the market. Here you look at whether or not the particular offering is relevant to the transformation your business is ultimately creating in the world.

2. Inspiration:

Here you evaluate your product or service for the level of excitement, inspiration and motivation it ignites in you personally. If you're going to build a Profit Business Model to reach Freedom, you must be inspired by what you're offering in your business that you're personally exchanging your time to fulfill against. Remember, in a Profit Business Model the highest value is in your personal time and you need to ensure that where you are spending your time is bringing in the highest profit. Therefore, if your Freedom is based on increasing your profit for your time, then you'll want to be spending your time in the ways your most enjoy. Without this, trying to grow your business, particularly a profit business, is just hard. If you're building a Legacy Business Model then this also directly relates, just at a lesser intensity given that you are going to be focused on leveraging your involvement out of each product and service so that you can ultimately sell the business. You may be able to notice however, the products and services you want to leverage yourself out of faster than others. By doing this, work never becomes stale for you, and you influence more people because you're committed at the highest level to bring your unique value to the world.

3. Automation:

Here you evaluate how effectively your product or service can be marketed, sold and fulfilled without you. In the ideal scenario for a Profit Business Model everything is automated except for your higher dollar cost activities that you are most passionate about, which is where you are spending your time. For a Legacy Business, full automation is required across the entire business. It must be setup to run 100% without needing you.

4. Profit:

Finally you evaluate the profitability of each product or service. Profit is crucial here! There is a huge difference between profit and revenue. Your products must be profitable in such a way that they will allow you to create your Freedom. Whether that's through pulling profits out along the way (Profit Business Model) or building the assets in your business that will eventually sell at the highest value (Legacy Business Model).

That's the four criteria to create your "Magical Mix of Products" that sets you free. By evaluating your products and services based on the four criteria, you ensure you're truly set to build your Financial Freedom. You're creating the greatest impact in the world; you're fully lit up and inspired as you build your business. Not only that, you're only doing activities that matter (or what's essential to leverage yourself out of the business) and you're fully profitable in such a way that your Freedom becomes an inevitable end result! Next, we're going to take a moment to define the 5 different types of products. After you have an understanding of the five different types of products, you'll be able to see which category your current products and services fit under. Then, you'll view each of your products and services in a certain way. You're going to rate how well each product or service matches the criteria we just shared. As a result of that rating system, you'll see which services and products are best to focus the most amounts of time and energy on.

Criteria #1 - #3 are fairly intuitive. Unlike the previous two Chapters, there aren't as many numbers to calculate. You just follow the process and end up with a clearly customized plan for building your Freedom Generator through your products and services. Criteria #4 (Profit) requires some calculations. If you'd like a downloadable tool to help you with the process you'll learn here, see the Additional Resources page at the back of the book, or join the business owner community at MindShift.money. Okay! Let's get to the five different types of products…

The 5 Product Types

Product Type #1 - Packaged Products

Whether it's cereal, electronic ear buds, a DVD, a cellphone, or a digital camera, we define those items as Packaged Products. Packaged products aren't necessarily always physical though. They can also be delivered through an online medium, for instance a cooking course you pay a one-time fee for and can access for life. Even though it's not in a package, it is packaged for sale as one self-contained unit. Hence, we still define that as a packaged product. The delivery mechanism you use of a packaged product could be an online program the customer pays upfront or through a payment plan.

Product Type #2 - Continuity

This is anything subscription-based. You charge an ongoing monthly or annual payment for a service the customer uses (usually) each month. The value could come from information you provide your subscribers, for instance an SEO expert who shares information about the latest changes with Google Search Algorithms. Or another example is people who are part of our MindShift.money community. Among many other benefits, our "tribe" receives monthly updates on how to allocate their money in order to secure their Freedom.

Subscription services could be hardware/software related too. Using the same example, maybe that SEO expert also has a dashboard that tracks search ranking all in one place. Other examples include your CRM (customer relation management), or landing page software. Most of those companies are subscription based, instead of being packaged for one-time purchase.

The value of subscription could also lie within discounts you receive on products/services. Like with an Amazon Prime Membership you're guaranteed shorter delivery time (benefit #1) and you get discounts on shipping costs (benefit #2). For those benefits you pay a fee each year.

Product Type #3 - A Partner Product

This is a product you coproduce with someone else. Often this is a great way to create a strategic alliance with someone, the byproducts of which aren't just sales, but also access to a new customer base. Essentially, this is a product that splits profits between two or more people. Let's say Bob is a real estate agent and Sue is a social media expert. They may create a cobranded product called Social Media for Real Estate Agents. Once they build the product together, they agree to split the resulting profits by 50% to each of them. In order to successfully make this model work you have to be aware of your Freedom Number and make sure that the price of the service or the volume of sales is actually in alignment with your Freedom. A partnership can sound attractive because with two people you multiply the leverage. However, at the same time you can also multiply the complexity, which can decrease the yield you end up producing from the project.

Product Type #4 - Affiliate Product

This is where you offer your client base a product produced by someone else, and then when they buy it you receive a commission. Some business models make their main source of profit from affiliate promotions to their existing prospect or customer lists. The affiliate becomes efficient at building their own prospect list, and then finds new products and services that other people have built to fulfill their list's wants, needs and desires. However, there is a warning to keep in mind with this too. It's lovely to have a list of people you can send an external offer to, receive a commission if they buy it, plus have none of the delivery costs associated with the product. That sounds great, right?

The potential downside of making too many of those offers is that it can dilute the credibility you maintain with your customers and decrease your sales in other areas. This depends on how you set up your model and what it is that your customers are expecting AND wanting to receive from you. Affiliate promotions are not bad or wrong. It's important to evaluate whether they are effective based on the impact you want to create. That is the ultimate filter for whether something is worth moving forward on or leaving behind.

Product Type #5 - Coaching and Consulting

This is where you're sharing your intellectual property one-on-one or in groups, helping people customize solutions for problems they have. In most cases, in order to get paid for this you have to personally show up to do it. You have to fulfill using your time.

Live Certification Courses, VIP Days, Boardroom Mastermind Meetings, and One-on-One Mentoring… All of those fall into the Coaching/Consulting Product and Service category. Not all coaching/consulting models require your time to fulfill. Some have created a framework for other people to become practitioners, incorporating leverage into the service. An excellent example is Landmark Education.

Categorize Your Products and Services

Now that you have an understanding of the different types of products and services, we're going to dive deeper into the criteria that help you get your Magical Mix of Products. As you read the following list of criteria, keep your current products and services in mind. A filtering process will naturally occur. You'll begin to see which of your products and services you should place more attention on going forward and which ones have more or less relevance to your Freedom. Also, as the saying goes, "don't throw the baby out with the bathwater," if you rate a product low based on one of the following criteria, that doesn't mean you should decide to immediately stop offering it in the marketplace. For instance, if you're not Inspired (Criteria #2) about a service you exchange your time to deliver right now (like coaching), but discover that if you could automate it (Criteria #3), then your passion may suddenly rise to a 10 out of 10! So, view this process as a holistic filtering system. One part is not more or less significant than another. They are equally important to establish your Magical Mix. Now it's time to evaluate each product and service to find out which will bring your Freedom closer.

Magical Mix of Products Criteria #1: Impact "How 'in line' is this product with the overall impact my business is set to create in the world?"

Ray Anderson was a shining icon for entrepreneurial vision, purpose and impact. He was the CEO of a company called Interface™, a carpet-tile manufacturer from Atlanta, Georgia. They are still the world's largest manufacturer of modular carpet for commercial and residential applications. In the summer of 1994, something happened to Ray Anderson that would change his life's direction, sense of significance and the direction of his company Interface™ forever. Traditionally, manufacturing carpet is an extremely toxic industry to the environment. They rely heavily on oil to produce the product, and then after they sell it: eventually it gets thrown into a landfill. The business model is: Take from the earth, Make the product and Waste it. Before the summer of 1994, Ray Anderson either wasn't conscious of, or he didn't care about terms like: Ecological Sustainability. To

151

him, environment meant a nice place to take a vacation. Then he read Paul Hawkens' book, "The Ecology of Commerce," and the clouds parted casting 'rays' of sunshine. In the book, Paul names business and industry as, one, the major cause of damage to our biosphere, and, two, the only community large enough to direct us onto a sustainable path. Paul also directly refers to Ray Anderson as: "A plunderer of the earth." (Yikes... Talk about 'Calling Bullsh*t') That's when everything changed for Interface™.

Instead of ignoring Paul's claims, reacting with a lawsuit, or blindly discrediting the accusations – instead: Ray listened. Then he broke down in tears. He thought of his grandchildren having to live in a toxic wasteland that he contributed to with his company. Ray committed to make a change. He even hired Paul Hawkens as one of his advisors on the board of Interface™. Ray made it his mission, purpose, passion and vision to: "Become 100% bio sustainable by the year 2020." Once he made that commitment, EVERYTHING in Interface's product-line was directed to support that vision. In fact, everything in their entire business model shifted. For instance, instead of selling the tiles, they rented them for a term, and then brought them back to their facilities to recycle the old fabrics into new ones. This changed the cash flow of their business, while reducing expenses and increasing profit.

They developed new technologies that made carpet from biodegradable sources. They used landfill gas emissions to fuel new production. Their annual meetings showed how much progress the made toward their target of zero waste. Their whole company culture changed. Ray Anderson, by the end of his life, didn't shake hands in the boardroom: he hugged the people he was meeting with!

You can learn more by watching Ray's TED Talk, "The Business Logic of Sustainability." The Point is this: Earlier in this book we explored your vision, purpose, passion and desire. Do you remember what it is? When you exit your business or simply close its doors at the end of your working life, what impact in the world do you want your business to have created? What is fullest expression of your business in the world? Think about that for a moment and while you do, ask yourself the following question… "On a scale of 1 — 10, how well do my current products and services match with the fullest expression of my business's impact?" Are you – as Ray Anderson was – consciously matching your ultimate business vision to the products and services you bring to the world?

Which products are fundamental to creating that impact and which are not? For example, if you weren't offering Coaching and Consulting "Product A" any longer, would the fullest expression and potential of your business not be created?

Which products express that impact the most?

Can you improve your existing products to maximize your vision?

Are there products that are better left behind?

Magical Mix of Products Criteria #2: Inspiration
"How much does this product excite, motivate and _inspire_ me personally?"

Of the products and services you offer, which ones get you motivated, fascinated and fuelled with passion when you think about delivering and/or getting it into the hands of your customers?

This criteria is crucial if you are a building a Profit Business. The more passion you have around what you are offering, the more inspired you will be to get it out to as many people as possible and do what it takes to grow your business. In the case of a Legacy Business, passion around a specific product may not be as important. In our case, our passion comes more from our overall mission of reaching 20 million people and reaching a tipping point, more so than the passion we have around any particular product or offering itself.

Our mission at MindShift.money is to create a new normal in society where financial literacy is no longer reserved for only a small percentage of the population AND where Financial Freedom is normal. We want to statistically increase the ratio of people who become Financially Free. Passion is like the fuel that drives your entire business forward. So take some time to think about all your services and products and rate them. If you are building a Profit Business: Ask yourself these two simple questions:

- Of your products and services, which ones inspire you the LEAST to develop and fulfill against with your audience?
- Of your products and services, which ones inspire you the MOST to develop and fulfill against with your audience?

If you are building a Legacy Business: Ask yourself these two simple questions:

- Of your products and services, which ones inspire you the LEAST to bring to market?
- Of your products and services, which ones inspire you the MOST to bring to market?

Magical Mix of Products Criteria #3: Automation
"How automated is this product? Can it run completely without me?"

This criteria involves an understanding of the difference between automation and delegation. Automation is the ability to use technology or anything that allows the work to be complete with no effort required by a person. Examples of this could be software that delivers a digital product automatically or a sales page that does the selling for you. With automation, there is no effort required by yourself or your team members. Delegation is having someone on your team whether an employee or contractor, that performs tasks for you. With delegation, there is no effort or time required by you as someone else is completing the task. Now that you understand this, lets dive into Criteria #3. Within this criteria, you will need to evaluate each product or service you offer to see how well it can run completely without you (automation and delegation combination). In order to do this you must evaluate each product and service for the following:

1) Development – Is this product already developed or do I need to still create it?
2) Marketing and Sales – Can the marketing and selling of this product be completely run without me or does it need any involvement from me to market and/or sell?
3) Fulfillment – Is this product completely evergreen (it runs on its own and doesn't need any human involvement to

fulfill against the product promise) or does it require ongoing time, effort or energy to fulfill against once it has been sold?

Once you have asked these questions against each product you can then rate each product out of 10 (being totally automated and/or delegated and needs 0 of my involvement right now). Typically, in a Profit Business Model no product or service you offer will be completely automated (10/10). However, The aim would be to completely automate and/or delegate any activity that is not in your highest value of your time. You only want to be performing task and activities that sit as your highest dollar cost activity or bring the greatest fulfillment. In a Legacy Business Model, your aim would be to have each product and service fully automated, or a combination of fully automated and delegated. You need to have no involvement in the development, marketing, selling or fulfilling of the product or service in your business to be able to effectively sell it for the highest value.

When we did this exercise, if we didn't rate a product a 10/10 for automation then we took an extra step to increase our clarity. We wanted to get clear on what part of the product or service was not currently automated or delegated.

Of each product, we wrote down every part of the development, marketing, selling and fulfilling that currently needed us. Next to each one we then decided whether we could totally automate it (meaning it needed no human involvement to run) and which parts we needed to delegate (it needed human involvement, but not ours).

For a Legacy Business Model you need to be able to automate and delegate every part of the process. For a Profit Business, you would run the same exercise here but you would look to automate and delegate every activity that wasn't the highest value of your time, so you are left doing only the highest dollar cost activities.

This process will also reveal to you which products and services are currently super efficient, and potentially deserve more attention to promote because of their ease. Consider these key factors and allow them to influence your Magical Mix of Products!

Magical Mix of Products Criteria #4: "How Profitable (or un-profitable) is this product? How aligned is it with my Freedom?"

Pricing has the tendency to be a big stumbling block for many entrepreneurs. They set their prices based on how other people in their industry price their services. Or worse: they create their prices randomly, basing them on hope or a 'feeling' their clientele will accept their prices. The first thing to remember about pricing is that you're not basing prices on, "someone said so." We can't count the number of seminars we've gone to where a person asks a question about price and a random answer comes from the audience: "You should sell it for $1,000!" Well, hold on a second. What if it costs more than $1,000 to get that sale and to fulfill against it? Well, now you're at a loss, so what's the point in pricing it at $1,000 just because someone says it will sell for that? Or what if the product is better suited to sell for $1 instead of $1,000. It all depends on the business model you have chosen for your vision, as well as your Freedom Goals. In order to help you prevent those pricing mistakes we designed a formula to determine the perfect prices every single time. The formula is called The Perfect Price Calculator.

159

The reason this calculator can identify your *"perfect"* prices is because it incorporates your Freedom Number into your pricing model. That means your prices directly relate to build a big enough Freedom Generator that produces your Freedom Number in passive income. What could be more perfect than knowing every sale you make is directly linked to your Freedom? Before we walk you through the process to use your Freedom Number to set your prices, it's important for you to understand the following concept... Know Your *Pricing Pyramid.*

On August 5, 2004, Wharton School Published a book by a man named C.K. Prahalad entitled, The Fortune at The Bottom of The Pyramid — Eradicating Poverty Through Profits. The premise of the book is that you can change the scale of products and services (and/or innovate them for different conditions) so they can be sold even to people who live on less than $1 each day. This raises their standard of living and creates new opportunities and innovation for everyone. Hindustan Unilever™ produced one of the products that emerged from those innovations; a shampoo that works best in cold water. They come in palm-sized, individual packages, which reduces the barriers of upfront costs to the poor. What the financially poor people lack in money, they gain in their volume. So, if you can sell one million of something for one dollar each: you have a million dollars of revenue. With Bottom-of-The-Pyramid-type-thinking: one may not raise their prices – they may lower them! However, they direct their attention toward an audience that is larger in scale. As a result, they increase the amount of volume of sales; reach more people, and earn more money. The opposite is also a viable way to think about your pricing... Let's say – to keep this simple – your Freedom Generator goal is $2,000,000.00. What if you could sell ONE something for two million-dollars? Depending of your profit margins, you could be set with as little as 1 or 2 sales! While keeping this price design in mind, on the next section we're going walk you through the steps to create your Perfect Pricing.

First we'll run through a quick example, and then you'll follow the same steps to create your perfect pricing structure...

Exercise #1:

PERFECT PRICE CREATOR				
MINIMUM PROFIT NUMBER: (per month)			IDEAL PROFIT NUMBER: (per month)	
$13,333			$21,667	
PRODUCT	PRICE	COST	PROFIT	Number of Sales needed?
How to Course	$497	$100	$397	????

In order to keep this first exercise super simple we're going to treat your business as if you only have one product to sell – a 'How to Course'. That way, you can see how that product's sales would relate to your other products and services and your Minimum Profit Number and Ideal Profit Number (using the average monthly profit numbers from our example in the previous chapter).

As you can see, there are two factors at the top:
1. Your Ideal Profit Number; and
2. Your Minimum Profit Number

Your freedom aligns to you reaching your Profit Numbers; which in turn determines how you need to customize your Pricing, Number of Products, Cost and number of sales required.

Also, we'd like to caution you about how we are defining "Cost" in this equation. This isn't just the cost of production. It's also the Cost of Sale. One of the big problems business owners make when they calculate their prices is: projecting as if they keep all of that money. Commissioned sales reps, entrepreneurs and, heck, fishermen know what "net return" means more than anyone else. It's not what you make that counts, it's what you keep. Cost of Sale is essentially the total amount of money it costs you to gain a new customer. Without determining your cost of sale (in addition to) your cost of production/fulfillment, you're not taking all the numbers into account. Determining this is the only way to accurately calculate your profit per unit sold. Depending on how cash flows through your business, the way you determine your Cost of Sale may vary. However it could be as simple as taking what you spend on marketing each year and dividing that number by the amount of new clients you gained that year. Your cost of sale will likely also be different for each product/service you offer.

So, lets get back to this example. The question for this exercise is this: how much volume (how many units) do you need to sell each year in order to reach your Minimum Profit Number and then your Ideal Profit Number? In this example I'm going to be using the Ideal Profit Number only. The aim is to secure your freedom as soon as possible, right? So let's see what you have to do reach it. The calculation is quite simple.

You take your Profit Number target and divide it by how much profit per unit you make on that product.

$21,667 (Ideal Profit Number)

/

$397 (profit/unit)

=

55

Therefore, you need to sell 55 units per month to make $21,667 profit! So, what if you increase or decrease your price for that product? Assuming your costs stay the same, how does that impact your volume of sales you need to make now to reach Freedom?

What would happen if you doubled the price to $997 per unit, and the cost stayed at $100, leaving you with a profit of $897 per unit? You take your Profit Number target and divide it by how much profit per unit you make on that product.

$21,667 (Ideal Profit Number)

/

$897 (profit/unit)

=

24

Therefore, you now need to sell 24 per month to make $21,667 profit. Doubling your prices in this example reduces the number of products you need to sell by more than half (56% to be exact)! Now, what would happen if you cut the price in half to $249 per unit, and the cost stayed at $100, leaving you with a profit of $149 per unit?

You take your Profit Number target and divide it by how much profit per unit you make on that product.

$$\$21,667 \text{ (Ideal Profit Number)}$$

$$/$$

$$\$149 \text{ (profit/unit)}$$

$$=$$

$$145$$

Therefore, you now need to sell 145 per month to make $21,667 profit. Halving your prices in this example increases the number of products you need to sell by <u>264</u>%! Don't get too caught up in the details of the math. Firstly, these are just examples. Secondly, the purpose of these calculations is for you to understand if you change one number: it affects the rest. In addition, we want to reaffirm the most important part of these calculations is this: "Your Freedom Always Comes First."

Your personal financial freedom must be built into your business plan. Your Minimum Profit Number and Ideal Profit Numbers have been carefully considered to ensure that you will build your Freedom Generator within your Maximum Freedom Timeframe and your Ideal Freedom Timeframe respectively. This is your Truth…and these numbers are your True North! You are like the architect of your universe. You can adjust your Products, Prices,

Volume of Sales and Number of Products; however they must align to your True North...non-negotiable! If this is the only insight you get from The Customize Phase – "base your prices on Freedom first" – then you are virtually guaranteed to become Financially Free. In the next exercise, we're going to incorporate ALL your products and services to see the full scope of your pricing model as it relates to your Freedom. Then you're going to customize it to create your Perfect Prices.

Exercise #2:

For this illustration, we're going to look at your business as if your freedom number will be achieved through selling an equal ratio of products and services. Meaning, if you think of your Profit Number as a single pie and the total number of products and services as the number of times you slice that pie; we are going to make each slice equal in proportion. In reality, it's likely that one product/service will have far more impact (bigger slice) on your Profit Number than others do. The reason it's important to see your business in this way is because it clearly outlines the volume of sales you need to achieve your Profit Number for products and services of high or low price points. This is like a calibration process. It places everything in a balance, and then you adjust your numbers according to which Products/Services you want to place more weight. We've also included a worked example towards the end of this chapter.

CALCULATE VOLUME – STEP #1				
PROFIT NUMBER	**/**	**TOTAL NUMBER OF P/S**	**=**	**TOTAL PROFIT NEEDED PER P/S**
	/		**=**	

PERFECT PRICE CALCULATOR	
MINIMUM PROFIT NUMBER: (per month)	**IDEAL PROFIT NUMBER:** (per month)

PRODUCT	PRICE	COST	PROFIT	SALES Min.	SALES Ideal
1.					
2.					
3.					
4.					
5.					

SERVICES	PRICE	COST	PROFIT	SALES Min.	SALES Ideal
1.					
2.					
3.					
4.					
5.					

1. **First,** list your Minimum Profit Number and your Ideal Profit Number. Then, list all your products and services that you currently offer.
2. **Next,** add the number of your products and services together (e.g. if you have 4 products and 2 services: you total 6).
3. **Now,** take your Profit Number and divide it by the Total Number of Products and Services (P/S). This gives you the total amount of profit you need to generate per product/service in order to hit your Profit Number.

4. **Lastly,** take the Total Profit Needed and divide it *individually* by the number of profit each product/service earns. This will give you the volume of sales each product and service you need to sell. Do this for your *Minimum Profit Number* and again for your *Ideal Profit Number.*

CALCULATE VOLUME – STEP #2				
		AMOUNT OF PROFIT PER PRODUCT		**VOLUME of SALES NEEDED TO HIT PROFIT NUMBER**
		1.		1.
		2.		2.
		3.		3.
TOTAL PROFIT NEEDED PER P/S:	**/**	4.		4.
		5.	**=**	5.
		SERVICE PROFIT		**VOLUME of SALES NEEDED TO HIT PROFIT NUMBER**
		1.		1.
		2.		2.
		3.		3.
		4.		4.
		5.		5.

EXAMPLE OF MAGICAL MIX OF PRODUCTS:

As promised, here is a worked example:

PERFECT PRICE CALCULATOR				
MINIMUM PROFIT NUMBER: (per month)		**IDEAL PROFIT NUMBER:** (per month)		
$13,333		$21,667		
PRODUCT	**PRICE**	**COST**	**PROFIT**	**VOLUME**
How to Course	$497	$100	$397	*SEE CHART BELOW*
Software	$5,000	$430	$4,570	
Merchandise	$49	$5	$44	

SERVICE	PRICE	COST	PROFIT	VOLUME
Mastermind	$10,000	$1,250	$8,750	*SEE CHART
Coaching	$1,000	$280	$720	BELOW*

CALCULATE VOLUME – STEP #1				
MINIMUM PROFIT NUMBER	/	TOTAL NUMBER OF P/S	=	MINIMUM PROFIT NEEDED PER P/S
$13,333				$2,667
IDEAL PROFIT NUMBER	/	5	=	IDEAL PROFIT NEEDED PER P/S
$21,667				$4,333

CALCULATE VOLUME – STEP #2					
TOTAL PROFIT NEEDED PER P/S:		AMOUNT OF PROFIT PER PRODUCT		VOLUME of SALES MIN. PROFIT NUMBER	VOLUME of SALES IDEAL PROFIT NUMBER
		$397		7	11
Minimum $2,667	/	$4,570	=	0.6	1
		$44		61	98
		AMOUNT OF PROFIT PER SERVICE		VOLUME of SALES MIN. PROFIT NUMBER	VOLUME of SALES IDEAL PROFIT NUMBER
Ideal $4,333		$8,750		0.3	0.5
		$720		4	6

"What do these numbers mean, and how should I adjust them to hit my Profit Number?"

The purpose of this exercise is to see which products and services have the highest leverage to make your Freedom a reality. In addition, which ones you should be paying more attention to bringing to market. The chart on the last page shows a business with a total of 5 products and services, each responsible for 1/5th of the total Profit Number. Look at the bottom right number in the chart above, "Coaching = 6." Having 6 monthly Coaching spots filled will produce 1 of 5 parts of our Ideal Profit Number. What if we doubled that number to 12? Then it would account for 2 of 5 parts! And we could eliminate the "Merchandise", which requires 98 sales in that same time. We could also increase the price of the Coaching, right? If the Coaching was $1,720 a month instead of $1,000, by still filling 6, it covers 2 of 5 parts of our Ideal Profit Number. This would allow us to eliminate the "Merchandise" from our list of products and still reach our Ideal Profit Number. But maybe we hate running Coaching. It's a pain in our butts and we'd prefer to get rid of it entirely. What could we do then? Could we sell 196 pieces of merchandise instead of 98? Maybe we change our price to $93 instead of $49? Either way would cover that 1 of 5 parts of our Freedom Number. In a way, the process of Freedom is easy as pie. Maybe we add a new product! Oh my! What happens then? We could lower all prices... Or keep them the same, but shorten our Freedom Timeframe. The point is this: Do you see how your Profit Number determines what your Prices are? Also, do you see how the Amount of Products and

Services you offer is related to your prices too? It's the same with your Volume of Sales and your Freedom Timeframes... ALL of those factors, when you calculate them with your Freedom Number become clear: pricing is a WHOLE-ISTIC system, not random.

Take some time right now to adjust your numbers and see how the Sales Volume changes compared to how you Price something. Make the process exciting. Again, if you hate actually doing the calculations manually, I invite you to join our business owner community over at MindShift.money, and get access to our Perfect Price Calculator. At MindShift.money, you will also be able to find coaches and advisers who can help you hands on with making sure you get these right for you. Either way: take the time to ensure your pricing is never a stumbling block for you again. Always consider your pathway to freedom and your Profit Number before you think about price. Never set your prices based on how other people in your industry price their services or products. It is COMPLETELY irrelevant to your Freedom. Make pricing a knowable process, not a random event. You'll find the more times you calculate your prices based on your own Profit Number, the more confidence you'll have when determining the right price points for your products and services.

CHAPTER 10

THE THIRD PHASE OF FREEDOM: MONETIZE

If you recall back to Chapter 6, we talked about how the underlying process of the 3 Phases of Freedom; Crystalize, Customize and Monetize; is similar to planning and taking a vacation to a tropical island. When you go on a vacation, the first things you do are: choose your destination and review how much money you can allocate to your trip. In the context of securing your Financial Freedom that same process translates into what we accomplished in the Crystalize Phase. After you define where you want to go on vacation, the next step is to plan how you're going to get there. For example, you look at hotels, rental cars, cool places you want to visit, etc. The planning process for a vacation is like the second Phase: Customize, in the context of Freedom… And now it's time for you to get on your flight, go on vacation, and most importantly: ENJOY YOUR JOURNEY. What we mean by take flight is that it's time for you to implement the plan you created from the last two Phases. "Implementation," "Tracking," and "Optimization," is the purpose of the Third Phase.

You're going to Implement your plan, Track your results, and Optimize your progress and performance until you achieve Freedom. In order to make sure you implement, track and optimize your Freedom the correct way: in this Chapter, you're going to take all the components of your plan and schedule them in your (and your team's) calendar and make them into a reality. Scheduling may not sound sexy, fun or fascinating. However, all the planning in the world won't do any good if those plans remain on paper. What you schedule will get done.

The great thing is you've already completed the majority of the heavy lifting in the last two phases. Meaning, through The Crystalize Phase and The Customize Phase, you established all the components you need to implement, track and optimize – in their correct order – so you can build your Freedom Generator within (at least) your Maximum Freedom Timeframe. Let's take a moment to review the summary of what those components are. If you'll recall, in the Crystalize Phase you accomplished the following 4 outcomes:

1. Your clarified your personal Baseline Lifestyle Number
2. You calculated your Freedom Number
3. You set your two Freedom Timeframes:
   - Your Maximum Freedom Timeframe
   - Your Ideal Minimum Freedom Timeframe

4. You set your two Profit Goals for Your Business (which covers your Personal Baseline Living Expenses and builds your Freedom Generator within your Freedom Timeframes). These were:
   - Your Minimum Profit Number
   - Your Ideal Profit Number

Then, in addition to those MASSIVE wins, in the Customize Phase you accomplished the following:

1. You defined the 5 Product Types:
   - Packaged Products
   - Continuity Programs
   - Partner Products
   - Affiliate Product
   - Coaching and Consulting
2. You established your Magical Mix of Products by filtering your current products through 4 criteria:
   - Being in line with your vision.
   - Your personal excitement.
   - How automated it is to deliver
   - Pricing your products to accomplish Freedom

So, the purpose of this Chapter is <u>not</u> how you're going to accomplish Freedom. It's not to establish why Freedom is important. It's also not about what you need to do in order to achieve Freedom. The purpose of this Chapter is to make sure you know <u>When</u> "The How, Why and What" gets complete over

time, and by <u>Whom</u> it's completed by. It's about making sure you make measurable progress in reasonable time!
So let's do it!

Schedule Your Dream Into Reality

The first things you'll want to ensure is that you schedule two types of Progress Reviews into your calendar. Basically, a Progress Review is time for you and your team to measure the progress you're making toward your goals so you can readjust accordingly, and most importantly: WIN!

There are two types of Progress Review: the first is your Monthly TACTICAL Review. We suggest that you set aside about 2 - 4 hours each month for this review. The second is your Quarterly STRATEGIC Review, which we suggest you allocate a whole day to once every 3 months. In case you're wondering: at the beginning of your Quarterly Strategic Review, you start by doing your Monthly Tactical Review. Meaning, you can the two sessions into one meeting. So let's talk about the criteria for each meeting. What is the difference, and how do you successfully implement each into your business for the best results?

These meeting are about making sure you are on track with the execution of your plans; and also allowing space for you to determine if or when your plans need to be adjusted for you to stay on course for your ultimate freedom destination. If you remember back to the last chapter, we talked about adaptive challenges and technical challenges in the context of automating parts of your business. Interestingly, those same two concepts are also the main difference between your Monthly Tactical Review and your Quarterly Strategic Review. Your Monthly Tactical Review is designed to adjust technical challenges that may be underperforming at that time. For instance, if you're running an ad campaign, you may review the "creative," which is: the headline you use, the images, the body copy, and/or the call to action. Then you'd design new creative to test in the following 30 days to see if you can incrementally improve that part of that technical process. However, often 30 days is not enough time for you to get the most accurate sense of whether tactics are in alignment with your entire Big Vision of the company. That's why each quarter you need a Strategic Review.

Thinking back to our vacation example, a Monthly Tactical Review is like adjusting the speed on your rental car so that you arrive at your destination on time. The Quarterly Strategic Review is about checking if you are still on the best route, or if there is a faster route to get you there. It may time to ditch the car in favor of a helicopter or plane. Remember the key is to be committed to reaching to your destination on time; not the vehicle you use to get there!

Your Quarterly Strategic Review is time for you to think about strategic shifts — changes to your focus, product mix or pricing; or fundamental changes to the business that you are in — that you can make to increase your value and impact in the marketplace. When we started MindShift.money, it was originally called The Freedom Club. Our destination and commitment was (and still is) to change the financial health of the planet. We started as a financial services business (because that was Tony's background), and it's often an easy decision to start with what you know. The further we moved down our journey, the clearer it became that this business vehicle was not going to get us to the destination that we were committed to. During one of our Quarterly Strategic Reviews we came to the conclusion that if we were seriously committed to reaching our destination, we needed to change vehicles. The strategic shift to a publication and digital education platform would be an exponentially stronger model to reach our destination. This would allow us to reach millions more people all around the world simultaneously; and in addition create a platform where we could collaborate with other experts and change-makers around the world who were also committed to seeing this change come into the world. So, we left our first vehicle to change to a much faster and more powerful vehicle. Our commitment to our destination was unchanged (if anything it was strengthened!); but our vehicle changed. The breakthroughs you'll architect during your Quarterly Strategic Review are not meant to incrementally increase your productivity (as altering a technical challenge does). The breakthroughs you'll architect during this Review influence your business exponentially. It's looking at what progressed your mission the furthest over the past 90 days (6 month, or even the year), and asking how you can multiply that by 2, 5, 10 times, then implement those shifts during the next 90 days. It's also about uncovering the ways you can eliminate what prevents you from progressing faster or more profitably. In the next section we're going to give you our step-by-step process to conduct each type of Review.

But wait! There's one little warning before you proceed. It's something that will likely sabotage 80% of the people who begin to implement their Monthly and Quarterly Reviews. This is a very real danger you must be aware of that could take you out before you even begin. It's called: "you're too busy." When people say something along the lines of: "I just don't have the time… I'm too busy to take time from work." We often respond (kindly) with the following… **That is total BS.** It's true: you are too busy… But the question is: busy doing what? If you're not busy getting Free, you're busy spinning your wheels and going nowhere fast. People who are busy getting Free make the time to review their progress toward their goal. Every single #1 champion athlete you could name spends hours upon hours reviewing his or her own performance: strategizing how to get an edge and win. That's what we want you to do. If there were a magic pill you could eat, that would eliminate the need for Review, we'd point you in that direction (right after we'd also taken it!). However, if your top priority is building your Freedom Generator in the real world, do the following…

1. Book your one-day Quarterly Strategic Review into your calendar. Consider scheduling this for the middle of the second week of each new quarter. This gives you time to have accurate numbers to review from the previous quarter.

2. Book your 2 - 4 hour Monthly Tactical Review into your calendar. Consider doing your review in the middle of the second week of each month. This gives you time to have accurate numbers to review from the previous month.

Terrific! Now we're going to walk you through the process to conduct those Business Reviews.

Our team at MindShift.money designed interactive and editable dashboards as a way to both facilitate our business reviews, and track, measure and optimize our performance each month, quarter and year. For this book, we've deconstructed parts of our dashboards so that:

  a) We can walk you through each one step-by-step.
  b) The format would fit so you can see them.

Due to limited space within these pages, we recommend you either recreate what you're about to see using a spreadsheet, or head over to the business owner community at MindShift.money and get access the tools we personally use. We began this book at the end: Your Freedom. Once again, we're beginning at the end. This is the top take-away for most people – what is unique about the process – is using your Freedom as the base for everything else in your business. At every Monthly and Quarterly Review, always begin by reminding yourself of the destination that you are working towards. The reviews are then about checking where you actually are along the journey to that destination compared to where you were planning to be. "What you measure you can manage!" So what do you measure? There are 9 strategic areas that you would be wise to monitor in this phase:

  1. Freedom First - begin at the end
  2. Profit/Loss Summary (Annual/Monthly)

3. Statement of Cash flows
4. Balance Sheet
5. Debts/Receivables (Annual/Monthly)
6. Magical Mix of Products (Monthly)
7. Magical Mix of Products (Annual)
8. Marketing Summary (Annual/Monthly)
9. Media Effectiveness (Monthly)

1. Freedom First - Begin At The End

Remember, your Freedom lies outside of your business. So the truest measuring stick for you ultimately being able to get enough money out of your business to secure your personal financial freedom is your Profit Numbers. You must get above your Minimum Profit Number as soon as possible, and aim to get above your Ideal Profit Number as quickly as you can. These are the truest measuring stick for success in ALL your other tracking. Naturally, since everything else we'll measure is on the "year, quarter, month" basis, you'll take your Profit Number and divide it into the amount of profit you need to generate in those time periods. For simple illustration:

#1: BEGIN AT THE END		
YOUR FREEDOM GENERATOR:	IDEAL FREEDOM TIMEFRAME:	MAXIMUM FREEDOM TIMEFRAME:
$2,000,000	10	20
ANNUAL PROFIT NUMBER:	$160,000	$260,000
QUARTERLY PROFIT NUMBER:	$40,000	$65,000
MONTHLY PROFIT NUMBER:	$13,333	$21,667

You've got the end in mind. Next it's time to review the summary of your Profit and Loss statements.

2. Profit/Loss Summary (Annual/Monthly)

In Chapter 7 and Chapter 8, we covered how to account for the individual expenses, profit, debt, sales, etc. of your business. So with this Dashboard you've collected the high-level SUMMARY of your business's current financial state.

#2: YOUR PROFIT & LOSS SUMMARY						
	ACTUAL			GOAL		
MONTH	PROFIT	REVENUE	EXPENSES	PROFIT	REVENUE	EXPENSES
QUARTER #1						
JANUARY:						
FEBRUARY:						
MARCH:						
QUARTER #2						
APRIL:						
MAY:						
JUNE:						
QUARTER #3						
JULY:						
AUGUST:						
SEPTEMBER:						
QUARTER #4						
OCTOBER:						
NOVEMBER:						
DECEMBER:						
TOTAL:						

*Note: You should be able to easily access this report from your financial software. We highly recommend that you place a high priority on having your bookkeeping up-to-date using an online system like QuickBooks Online or Xero that link to direct data-feeds from your bank accounts. The first thing you want to do is insert your "monthly profit number" into the GOAL column under "profit", in the next month's row. Then calculate your revenue goal and your expenses goal. Keep in mind the purpose of the second step is not to strategize about how you're going to solve, improve or optimize your numbers. You simply want to be as accurate as possible. ESPECIALLY in regard to "what your profit actually is."

At your Monthly Tactical Review, you'll begin by looking at your goal from the previous month, and then compare that with what your actual results were for the month. The idea is for you to use these numbers to see where you are on-track and where you are off-track. Where you're off-track, you want to look deeper into what actions will increase revenue while decreasing your expenses, and thus increase your net profit. The aim, again, is to make measurable progress in reasonable time. This is how you measure your progress, and the time it is taking you to make that progress. Become a razor sharp, samurai for knowing what your NET numbers are, at all times. This is the life-blood of your business. Every year we meet people who are celebrated in public for their "great, $500,000 or $1,000,000 launch," or what sounds to be a BIG win. Then, in a couple of conversations it becomes clear: they spent $100,000 on ads, $50,000 on development costs, another $25,000 on staff. Then they paid out their affiliate and joint venture partners... And very often, they had nothing or very little that they personally received from these big revenue launches ... AND STILL had the additional back-end costs of delivering the goods and refunds or failed payment plans. Now, we're not saying to avoid launching a product. It's just important to illustrate that what your business earns in revenue is not the same what you personally really earn from your business.

So, make sure your numbers are a true reflection of Net profit... Not gross; not revenue; not clicks; not leads; not accounts payable; none of that. "Net Profit numbers" are the only that matters to our Financial Freedom.

3. Statement of Cash flows

So what is a Statement of Cash Flows, and how is it different to a Profit and Loss statement? Basically, a (monthly) Profit and Loss statement will show you the sales you made for the month, and the invoice (expenses) you received for the month. But just because you made a sale doesn't mean that you actually received some or all of the money from that sale into your bank account in the same month. The same goes for expenses. Just because you bought something doesn't mean that you paid all or some of the money out of your bank account the same month. Why is this important?

Well, because actual cash flowing into and out of your bank accounts is the lifeblood of your business. It is important to know how much money actually came into your bank account, and how much money left your bank account during the month/quarter/year.

The Statement of Cash flow shows you this... Below is a simplified version for monitoring purposes (it only looks at money flowing in and out from sales and expenses (a full statement of cash flow also looks at money for investing and financing).

#3: STATEMENT OF CASHFLOWS		
CASH FLOW FROM OPERATING ACTIVITIES	ACTUAL	GOAL
1. CASH RECEIVED FROM SALES		
2. CASH PAID TO SUPPLIERS AND EMPLOYEES		
NET CASH FLOW FROM OPERATING ACTIVITIES (1-2)		

*Note – this, again, is a simple report from your bookkeeping software. Ask your accountant/bookkeeper to make sure this is set up correctly for you.

4. Balance Sheet

Your Balance Sheet is like a dam of water a community relies on for a steady supply of drinking from You will have water flowing into the dam (from sales), and water flowing out of the dam (expenses and your personal income you are paid from the business). However it is equally important that you monitor the level of water in the dam. If the water level in the dam fall below a critical level (suggest that this is a minimum of 3 months of operating expenses for your business) you need to pay attention to either increasing the flow of water into the dam (increase profitable sales), or reduce outflow (decrease or delay expenses) in the short term so that the dam can fill up to a healthy level again. Your Balance sheet shows you 3 readings:

1. Bank Account Balances (How much water is in your dam)
2. Current Assets/Receivables - how much money you are owed in the short term (think of this like how much water you are expecting to flow into your dam over the next month/quarter)
3. Current Liabilities/Payables - how much money you

currently owe to others (think of this like how much money you know will flow out of your account over the next month/quarter)

Below is a simplified version for monitoring purposes (it is likely that the statement you receive looks more detailed that this. However, these are the areas for you to be paying the most attention to on a monthly basis.)

#4: BALANCE SHEET		
	ACTUAL	GOAL
1. CASH		
2. ACCOUNTS RECEIVABLE		
3. ACCOUNTS RECEIVABLE		
TOTAL CURRENT NET ASSETS (1 + 2 - 3)		

5. Debts/Receivables (Annual/Monthly)

The next thing you want to see is how much money you owe and how much money is owed to you. Tracking your debts is how you gain an accurate view on your real expenses each month. In addition, your Receivables give you an accurate read into your real monthly cash flow. In the bottom right corner of the Receivables category you'll see "% 30 Day +." What that means is the percentage of people who owe you past this months tracked income.

That's important to know because, for instance, if a person buys something on a payment plan and the total amount of what they bought is $1,000: they haven't actually paid that amount, even though your books may say $1,000 owed. The cash that actually flowed into your business may only be $300. You want to see a balance between what's payable this month and what's actually coming in to your business. It is important to monitor that you are being paid what you are owed on a timely manner. Have good systems and procedures in place to send out reminders and follow-up to ensure you receive the money you are owed. Equally it is important that you pay your debts as and when they are due.

#5: YOUR DEBTS AND RECEIVEABLES					
– MONEY YOU OWE –					
WHO	AMOUNT OWED	MIN. MONTHLY PAYMENT	MONTHLY INTEREST AMT.	INTEREST RATE	MONTHLY DUE DATE
TOTAL:					
+ MONEY OWED TO YOU +					
WHO	AMOUNT OWED	MONTHLY PAYMENT	MONTHLY DUE DATE	% 30 DAY+	% 60 DAY+	% 90 DAY+
TOTAL:						

Between your Freedom Number; Profit/Loss Statement;

Statement of Cash Flows; Balance Sheet; and your Debts/Receivables, you have the "top of the mountain overview" of your business' financial health.

6. Magical Mix of Products (Monthly)

The next thing you want to know is how each individual product is contributing to those financial numbers. This sixth step is where you're taking your overview and making it more granular. The main things to pay attention to are the products/services that are responsible for the highest ratio of profit gained in relation to your monthly, quarterly and annual profit targets. In other words, you want to know which products and services are giving you the largest slice of Freedom Pie! You also should be concerned with products and services that are underperforming, or bringing the lowest ratio of profit in relation to your Freedom Plan. If you're allocating time and money to something that isn't bringing your expected return, you need to have those on your radar and adjust course accordingly. In your Quarterly Strategic Review, that's where you're taking time to think of ways to amplify the products and services that bring in the highest ratio of profit. Plus you want to either transform or even eliminate products that are not making measurable progress toward your targets.

#4: YOUR MAGICAL MIX OF PRODUCTS (MONTHLY)

DATE_____

PRODUCTS	PRICE	COST	PROFIT	ACTUAL VOLUME	GOAL VOLUME
1.					
2.					
3.					
4.					
5.					
6.					
7.					
8.					
9.					
10.					
SERVICES	PRICE	COST	PROFIT		
1.					
2.					
3.					
4.					
5.					
6.					
7.					
8.					
9.					
10.					

7. Magical Mix of Products (Annual)

This next chart enables you to track the summary of each product's profit for a full year. In the "A" slot you place what your Actual production was versus your "G" slot, which is your Goal. This is especially useful to review at your year's end.

#5: YOUR MAGICAL MIX OF PRODUCTS (ANNUAL)

Actual Total Profit Per Product VS. Goal Total Profit Per Product

PRODUCTS	JAN		FEB		MAR		APR		MAY		JUN		JUL		AUG		SEP		OCT		NOV		DEC	
	A	G	A	G	A	G	A	G	A	G	A	G	A	G	A	G	A	G	A	G	A	G	A	G
1.	A	G	A	G	A	G	A	G	A	G	A	G	A	G	A	G	A	G	A	G	A	G	A	G
2.	A	G	A	G	A	G	A	G	A	G	A	G	A	G	A	G	A	G	A	G	A	G	A	G
3.	A	G	A	G	A	G	A	G	A	G	A	G	A	G	A	G	A	G	A	G	A	G	A	G
4.	A	G	A	G	A	G	A	G	A	G	A	G	A	G	A	G	A	G	A	G	A	G	A	G
5.	A	G	A	G	A	G	A	G	A	G	A	G	A	G	A	G	A	G	A	G	A	G	A	G
6.	A	G	A	G	A	G	A	G	A	G	A	G	A	G	A	G	A	G	A	G	A	G	A	G
7.	A	G	A	G	A	G	A	G	A	G	A	G	A	G	A	G	A	G	A	G	A	G	A	G
8.	A	G	A	G	A	G	A	G	A	G	A	G	A	G	A	G	A	G	A	G	A	G	A	G
9.	A	G	A	G	A	G	A	G	A	G	A	G	A	G	A	G	A	G	A	G	A	G	A	G
10.	A	G	A	G	A	G	A	G	A	G	A	G	A	G	A	G	A	G	A	G	A	G	A	G

SERVICES																											
1.	A	G	A	G	A	G	A	G	A	G	A	G	A	G	A	G	A	G	A	G	A	G	A	G	A	G
2.	A	G	A	G	A	G	A	G	A	G	A	G	A	G	A	G	A	G	A	G	A	G	A	G	A	G
3.	A	G	A	G	A	G	A	G	A	G	A	G	A	G	A	G	A	G	A	G	A	G	A	G	A	G
4.	A	G	A	G	A	G	A	G	A	G	A	G	A	G	A	G	A	G	A	G	A	G	A	G	A	G
5.	A	G	A	G	A	G	A	G	A	G	A	G	A	G	A	G	A	G	A	G	A	G	A	G	A	G
6.	A	G	A	G	A	G	A	G	A	G	A	G	A	G	A	G	A	G	A	G	A	G	A	G	A	G
7.	A	G	A	G	A	G	A	G	A	G	A	G	A	G	A	G	A	G	A	G	A	G	A	G	A	G
8.	A	G	A	G	A	G	A	G	A	G	A	G	A	G	A	G	A	G	A	G	A	G	A	G	A	G
9.	A	G	A	G	A	G	A	G	A	G	A	G	A	G	A	G	A	G	A	G	A	G	A	G	A	G
10.	A	G	A	G	A	G	A	G	A	G	A	G	A	G	A	G	A	G	A	G	A	G	A	G	A	G

Once you know the effectiveness of each product in relation to your Profit Numbers, the next step is reviewing how those products and services are being sold.

8. Marketing Summary (Annual/Monthly)

To do this, you want to have a Summary Marketing Dashboard like the one below. This gives you a thumbnail sketch of how effective the combination of all your marketing methods are.

Each column is critical to know. You want to understand how much you spent on marketing; how many leads you got; what it cost to get a lead; how many of those leads converted to sales, and what those sales cost.

#6: YOUR ANNUAL MARKETING DASHBOARD					
MONTH	SPEND	# OF LEADS	COST / LEAD	# OF SALES	COST / SALE
QUARTER #1					
JANUARY:					
FEBRUARY:					
MARCH:					
QUARTER TOTAL:					
QUARTER #2					
APRIL:					
MAY:					
JUNE:					
QUARTER TOTAL:					
QUARTER #3					
JULY:					
AUGUST:					
SEPTEMBER:					

The Truth: THE REAL SECRET TO BUILDING A BUSINESS THAT SETS YOU FREE.

QUARTER TOTAL:					
QUARTER #4					
OCTOBER:					
NOVEMBER:					
DECEMBER:					
QUARTER TOTAL:					
GRAND TOTAL:					

*IMPORTANT: *You'll only know your "true" cost of sale within approx. 90 -180 days after their first enquiry (or opting into your list/campaign) . Often only a small % of people are ready to buy now and the remaining taking time and nurturing to begin to convert into a client. Think of marketing as a "capital investment". Think of marketing as a capital investment that is designed to pay you now and also later.*

Just as the anklebone is connected to the shinbone, which is connected to the knee: every one of the processes we've reviewed in these last moments are connected.

9. Media Effectiveness (Monthly)

This final Dashboard enables you to take your Marketing Summary and break down the effectiveness of each media (or lead source/funnel) you're currently using to attract and convert leads to sales.

Similar to your tracking your Magical Mix of Products, you want to view *which media source* is providing you with a positive return and bringing you closest to Freedom. If one form of media is more profitable than another, you'll be able to place more attention, energy and effort on that tactic.

#7: YOUR MONTHLY MEDIA DASHBOARD					
				DATE	
MEDIA	SPEND	LEADS	COST / LEAD	SALES	COST / SALE
FACEBOOK:					
TWITTER:					
PARTNERS/ AFFILIATES:					
YOUTUBE:					
GOOGLE:					
RADIO					
NEWSPAPER:					
TELEVISION					
DIRECT MAIL:					
SOLO ADS:					
SEO:					
LINKEDIN:					
TOTAL:					

During this chapter we set your Quarterly Strategic Business Review and your Monthly Tactical Review into your calendar. You also got 9 Tracking Dashboards to optimize your performance. Again, the summary of dashboards…

1. Freedom First - begin at the end
2. Profit/Loss Summary (Annual/Monthly)
3. Statement of Cash flows
4. Balance Sheet
5. Debts/Receivables (Annual/Monthly)
6. Magical Mix of Products (Monthly)
7. Magical Mix of Products (Annual)
8. Marketing Summary (Annual/Monthly)
9. Media Effectiveness (Monthly)

Those dashboards also serve as the process for your Business Reviews. Meaning, when you take the time at the end of each month to review your progress, you'll walk through each Dashboard in their same order.

Then, based on the data you see, you'll be able to get the best tactical and strategic answers to the following questions:

1. What's on track?
2. What not on track?
3. What should/could I do more of?
4. What should/could I do less of?
5. What should/could I stop doing?
6. What should/could I start doing?
7. Based on the above answers, what are my next steps?

Congratulations, you are officially Monetized. It's time now to go forward in the world and "Implement," "Track," and "Optimize," your performance until you secure your Freedom outside of your business, buy back your time and create a HUGE impact in the process. In the next chapter we're going to summarize the KEY POINTS that we covered during our time together. We're also going to show you where to access to the Additional Resources we made available to support you in your journey to Freedom.

PART III
YOUR NEXT STEPS

CHAPTER #11

FINAL THOUGHTS
& ADDITIONAL RESOURCES

At the beginning of this book we made a some promises to you. We promised to help you become conscious of every move you make in your business that have a financial impact and direct those actions to become Financially Free. That way you can maximize your impact in the world. We promised you tools, strategies and tactics to transform your business into an accelerator to your personal Financial Freedom. We promised to break down a step-by-step process that has been proven to work for entrepreneurs like you to create Financial Freedom in their lives. Through Part I and Part II of this book we followed through on our promises and gave you – not only the philosophy of creating Financial Freedom – but also the 3 Phases that enable you to:

- Crystalize what Freedom is for you.
- Customize your business to achieve it.
- Monetize your business and make Financial Freedom YOUR REALITY.

However, there's one thing we <u>did not</u> promise you. We did not promise Freedom is easy to *create*. Creating Freedom is simple.

Creating Freedom is straight-forward. Creating Freedom is attainable… But, it's not easy.

Human brains are hardwired to conserve energy, avoid pain and seek pleasure. All three of those things are counter to what it takes to succeed. Implementing your plan requires commitment, focus and dedication. It requires you to be willing to do things you may not be used to, and may be out of your comfort zone, to bring your plan into reality. It requires you to be mindful of not reacting to the changing winds of your emotions that could sabotage successfully implementing your Freedom plan. If 'success is a progressive realization of a worthy ideal,' then it is certainly the least "normal" realization one can progress toward. So, now it's time for you to create your new normal. It's time for you to – as the late, great Robin Williams quoted so beautifully – "Live deliberately… Live deep and suck out all the marrow of life. To put to rout all that was not life; and not, when I had come to die, discover that I had not lived" [Thoreau].

The Greatest Chance of Success

Worldwide, The Doors, have sold over one-hundred million albums, making them one of the best-selling bands of all time. When Jim Morrison, lead singer of The Doors, told his father he was going to travel across the country in a rock n' roll band, Jim's father scoffed at the idea and said, "That's ridiculous. You're not a singer. You can't sing. You are on the wrong track here. Get yourself a job!" Jim later remarked, "The most loving parents and relatives commit murder with smiles on their faces. They force us to destroy the person we really are: a subtle kind of murder." On your journey to Freedom, it's important to protect your mind from the outside forces that attempt to sabotage your success. You want to nurture your mind by surrounding yourself with people and information that supports you in achieving Freedom.

What if I need more help?

One question that we get a lot is: where you can go if you have more questions, or need more help and support. We have tried our best to give you clear strategies and solutions that can help you on the path to financial freedom, but obviously there is only so far that we can go within a book. It's one thing to learn, it's another to implement. That's why we created MindShift.money. MindShift.money is for you! It's the place where the 4% and the 96% come together and share for the benefit of us all. MindShift.money is an online publication, education platform and community where this very topic is at the heart of an open dialogue. Where there is empowering education, shared ideas and conversation on how we can all live engaged and enriched lives. Where the lessons of the privileged few to be available the everyone who wants to learn. In this book we examine the fundamental differences that separate the beliefs, knowledge, actions and ultimately lives of the 4% and the 96%.

At MindShift.money we're creating the bridge to bring everyone who wants to learn across to the world of the 4%. It is our deepest wish that we leave the world a better place for our families, communities and the generations that follow. Thousands of people from around the world are already part of the MindShift.money community. And just for you, we have custom tailored a special community for business owners only that has all the resources, tools and templates you need to complete the 3 Phases to Freedom. With others along side you who are devoted to doing the same. Plus, when you are a member of this community (only for business owners) we will gift you our 6 module program (Valued at $3997.00). Just go to http://mindshift.money/businessownersonly to get access to this now. We invite you to join us! This knowledge needs to be shared and taught to everyone. We have a huge job to do. Every voice counts...and we would love to hear yours! Join us in creating a new normal where there are way more than 4%

Financially Free and living their lives as they choose, and allowing their gifts to take full flight in the world. Let's create this world together!

Our last thoughts

"Always remember the reason you initially started working because there's something inside yourself that you felt, if you could manifest it in some way, you'd understand more about yourself and how you coexist with the rest of society."

-- David Bowie

You have a gift inside you. It's the impact you want to create in the world. We believe that your ability to fully express your impact in your world unlocks as a result of your Freedom. We believe in you. It's our highest priority to provide you with the precious elixir of information, knowledge and support that you need to unlock your Freedom. Thank you so much for being who you are. May your light shine brightly and leave a clear path for others to follow.

Tony & Makaylah

ABOUT THE AUTHORS

Dr. Tony Pennells, is a Best-Selling Author and Co-Founder of MindShift.money. He is the best-selling author of 3 books on finances and has built several businesses recognized by Business Review Weekly as the fastest 100 growing companies in Australia. Dr. Tony became financially free at 27 years old and was able to leave medicine to focus on being a husband to his amazing wife and father to two boys he calls "champions."

Makaylah Rogers, Co-Founder Chief Editor and CEO of MindShift.money. She is a Thought Leader for her generation, teaching people how to rewrite the "rules" we've been taught about money. With an extensive background in wealth building, Makaylah's path has taken her into several executive roles and positions across various fields including launching startups, real estate sales and motivational keynote speaking.

www.ingramcontent.com/pod-product-compliance
Lightning Source LLC
Chambersburg PA
CBHW021925190326
41519CB00009B/909